PREACHING IN A POST-TRUTH WORLD

I0807721

PREACHING IN A POST-TRUTH WORLD

Recentering the Pulpit in a Chaotic World

Mike Glenn

B&H PUBLISHING®
BRENTWOOD, TENNESSEE

Printed in the United States of America

979-8-3845-1187-8

Published by B&H Publishing Group
Brentwood, Tennessee

Dewey Decimal Classification: 251
Subject Heading: PREACHING \ SERMONS \ PASTORAL THEOLOGY

Cover design and illustration by Matt Lehman.
Background texture by Little River/Shutterstock.
Author photo by Lasting Media Group.

1 2 3 4 5 6 • 28 27 26 25

Contents

Foreword

When my kids were young, I coached their recreation league soccer teams before they were old enough to realize that Dad didn't know all that much about soccer, having grown up playing primarily baseball and basketball. It was a fun outlet, a great way to meet people in the community, and, as a preacher, a good form of cultural exegesis. My third daughter has always had a sweet spirit and a generous attitude, so she struggled one season as a five-year-old with my constant challenge to her to be more aggressive on the field. I'll never forget one bright sunny spring Saturday morning when suddenly mid-game it seemed to click for her. She attacked the ball, made a nice move to steal it from the other team, and broke away into free space in front of the goal. As everyone stood to their feet, she arced the perfect kick into the top corner of the net and past the goalie. The problem was . . . it was our own goalie! She had scored beautifully—in the wrong goal.

There is a problem with the effectiveness of our preaching today, and I often wonder if much of it has to do with the fact that we preach homiletically excellent sermons—but aim at the wrong net. We preach sermons aimed to placate members rather than engage the toughest questions of the lost. We preach sermons reacting to what we've seen on our social media echo chambers rather than based on one-on-one conversations with the hurting and confused in our community. We preach to the choir rather than counting the cost of truly speaking the truth in love.

In *Preaching in a Post-Truth World* my pastoral mentor and predecessor Mike Glenn makes a compelling case that while the gospel never changes, there is gap between our preaching and what people are hearing. When I led a group of fifty families to launch the first campus out of Brentwood Baptist Church fifteen years ago, Mike kept asking what I was learning as I preached and planted a congregation in a new community. After about a year, I was able to boil it down to one short phrase: *"Don't assume."* As we engaged a new community full of unchurched and de-churched people, I realized that we had made far too many assumptions. We assumed they had a basic understanding of the Bible. We assumed they understood our strategy. Most of all, we assumed they had heard the gospel clearly proclaimed and explained. Mike and I discussed, prayed, and planned how we would adjust our preaching to better connect with this new audience of often over-churched but tragically under-gospeled people.

As we added campuses and congregations to the Brentwood Baptist family over the years, our group of two became an entire room full of teaching pastors grappling with these same challenges. We had the privilege of hearing Mike unpack many of the truths he shares in this book and now you have the privilege of hearing and wrestling with them for yourself. Take them seriously. After serving under Mike's pastoral leadership for more than twenty years, I can tell you that he has the wisdom and experience to see through the trends and put his finger on the pulse of the congregation. Most importantly, Mike has a deep conviction that God uses both good preaching and dedicated preachers for God's glory and our joy. I'll never forget his repeated counsel to me: "Remember, there's a difference between delivering a sermon and preaching to people that you know and love."

With the help of the Holy Spirit, may this book help you to not only preach the right message but hit the right goal—the hearts and lives of the lost, confused, and searching in your mission field that Christ loves deeply and desires to come to a knowledge of the truth (1 Tim. 2:3–4).

Soli Deo Gloria,
Dr. Jay Strother
Senior Pastor
Brentwood Baptist Church

Introduction

There is a gap between the pulpit and the pew in our churches. To be honest, that's an understatement. There is a gap between the pulpit and the rest of the world. Those of us who proclaim the Word have usually done a lot of background work before we preach the sermon. I'm not talking about the exegesis required by the text of the sermon; I'm talking about the theological and philosophical background work that has led us to conclude that the Word of God is a reliable testimony and witness to the person, character—the ultimate reality—of God. When we hold the Scriptures before our congregations, we do so with the assurance that the truth we proclaim is strong and sure enough to build our lives on this foundation.

The ones in the pews aren't so sure. While the preacher is confident, the congregation is weighing the truth claims of the Bible against the truth claims they've been hearing all week. The community surrounding our churches is flooded with ads, opinions, and truth claims from various sources. The growth of social media means our congregations are engaged by thousands of truth claims every day. Most of these ads are harmless. They push everything from beauty care to the recent fashion trends. Others are more confrontational to the Christian message. Not only do the messages deny the Bible's truth, but they also question whether or not truth can be found at all. There are many secular theologians claiming there are many paths to God and many sources of truth. Truth is no longer universally verifiable, but simply a matter of individual taste.

More times than we care to admit, our congregations are responding to the Bible's claims of truth with a shrug that says, "Maybe."

This book is written to make sure our pastors know this gap is there. Assumptions we've made about how our people listen and process information are no longer valid. Social media platforms have destroyed our attention spans. These shortened attention spans mean people no longer make plans for next week or next month. They're simply trying to get through the day. The challenge these days isn't people believing the wrong things, but that people don't believe anything at all. I've spent a lot of time talking to these folks. They're not agnostic. They aren't atheists. They just haven't thought too much about it. It's like playing catch with someone who never throws the ball back. The people we're trying to reach aren't where we thought they were and they're not that interested in being reached.

If there is, indeed, a gap—and there is—how do we bridge that gap? The truth of the incarnation reminds us God closes the gap between our humanity and his divinity in the person of Jesus Christ. Preaching is an obedient response to the incarnation—the Word of God becoming flesh—in our living out the truth of Christ in real life, in real time. In a world where truth seems to be as malleable as Play-Doh, seeing the truth become real in a real life is a powerful message. The best preaching involves the whole person. Not just the sermon's words, but the life through which the sermon is delivered.

While these are indeed challenging times, I'm more confident about the future of the church than ever. Why? Because our world is asking questions only Jesus can answer. Questions of identity and purpose, meaning and hope—these are Jesus questions. These questions are answered in pulpits around the world by preachers who are preaching sermons with their whole lives, willingly laying their lives across the gap so that those who need to know can finally know the One who is the Truth.

If you've ever traveled on the trains in England, you're familiar with the conductor calling out, "Mind the gap." They're talking about the gap between the train car and the platform. If the passenger isn't paying attention, the gap can trip them as they're trying to get on or off the train. Preachers need to be mindful of the gap lest we inadvertently trip our congregations who are searching for the truth. While our first response may be that this challenge is too difficult, we will do well to remember the church has faced these same challenges before and has thrived. With God's help, we can thrive again.

Chapter 1

Looking for a Place to Stand

When I was growing up in Alabama, my family would vacation at the strip of Florida beaches between Panama City and Fort Walton affectionately called "The Redneck Riviera." As soon as we arrived at the beach, my friends and I were in the water. The older we got, the braver we became. Each year, we ventured further and further from the shore and, eventually, it happened. We found ourselves so far from the shore that the water was over our heads. We would push off the bottom and, the next moment, we would be gasping for air as our feet desperately prodded the void beneath us looking for the sandy bottom and a place to stand. We would swim back a few feet and try again. Sometimes, we would find bottom just after our faces had gone under water and we would bounce back up again and swim a little closer to shore. We'd try again, and if the water was still over our heads, we'd keep swimming toward the shore. Eventually, we'd find a place where we could stand with our heads above the water and bounce up and down above the waves.

I write this book having recently stepped down as a senior pastor. After more than forty-five years of congregational leadership, thirty-two of them at one church, I decided that it was time for me to do something else. I wanted to work with pastors and churches as they tried to figure out how to preach and serve in a world that seems to be unable to find the bottom. People in our world bounce up and down, gasping for air and trying to find a place where they can stand. Sooner or later, their heads slip under the waves, and they never come up again. As I continued in my teaching, preaching, and conversations with neighbors and friends, I noticed a change in their philosophies of life, their worldviews. To be honest, what I began to see wasn't a change as much as it was a disappearance of any coherent and thoughtful understanding of life or its meaning. I didn't find myself talking about faith with agnostics or atheists. These days, I was talking to people who didn't seem to have any theological foundations in their lives at all. They simply made decisions as they came up. If it worked out, fine. If it didn't, they would make another decision. There was no goal. There was no destination. There was no purpose. There was only today and the one goal of simply making it to the next. As I talked to my friends and acquaintances, most of them were happy I had found something that worked for me, but they either didn't see the benefit or feel the need to explore Christianity any further. I found myself feeling like I was at the beach again. I was bouncing up and down, trying to find the bottom. I couldn't find a place to stand. I couldn't find a place to begin.

This book is about finding a place to begin. Like missionaries of past generations, we find ourselves walking into a different country with a different language and culture. What worked "back home" in another place and another time won't work here and now. Where do we begin? Where do we start? We find ourselves missionaries in our neighborhoods. America is no longer a Christian nation. We have no statistic that would lead us to believe the citizens of the United States are mostly Christians. They may define their morality as based on "Judeo-Christian" values, but they wouldn't consider themselves to have surrendered to the lordship of Jesus Christ or committed to following his teachings.

Several years ago, my wife and I were enjoying a conversation with a couple we had met at a friend's home. They had just moved into the area and our hosts wanted to help them make some new friends in their new community. Our conversation led to the "what do you do for a living" question and our new friends were intrigued when they found out that I was the pastor of a Baptist church. (For some reason, interesting conversations always happen when people find out what I do for a living.) The husband wanted to know how I ended up in the ministry, and the answer to that question is my testimony (i.e., when I came to know Christ). This is what Christ wanted me to do with my life and I've been trying to live out his calling since that moment. The couple nodded and smiled politely, and the wife then said, "I'm glad you found your truth."

I didn't know what to do with her statement. The possessive pronoun caught me off guard. "*My* truth"? As far as I can remember, that was the first time I had heard someone use that phrase in ordinary conversation. I didn't know the truth was something that could be personally owned. I didn't know the truth could be personally validated. I believed truth was its own validation. I had always been taught and believed that truth existed outside of me. Truth stood on its own. I could accept the truth and live in alignment with that truth, or I could deny the truth and live with the consequences of my decision. Gravity is true and my denial of gravity doesn't stop gravity from reminding me of its power if I jump off a twenty-story building. I can deny gravity all I want, but gravity will teach me its truth in a brutal and definite fashion if I jump off the top of a building.

Yet, this wasn't the case for our new friends. For them, truth was something that helped them understand themselves and the world around them for the moment. They didn't agree with me. They didn't disagree with me. Both of them, husband and wife, just let my statements lie there. They didn't push back. In fact, there was no response at all. How do you play tennis if no one hits the ball back? For them, truth existed only in their own experience. What was real and what was good was determined by what worked for them in the moment. They had no need for their truth to be validated by any outside source. Everyone knows the sky is blue, right? Not necessarily. If my new friends had an experience where they thought the sky was green, then for them, the sky would always be green. Yes, I'm exaggerating, but not by much.

Let's take another example. The central issue around abortion seems to be when life begins. When does life become viable outside of the mother's womb? Or does life begin at conception? Most conservatives would agree with the latter assessment. The typical conservative talking points would be as soon as the woman's egg is fertilized, we have a human being. All the DNA that a baby will ever need is present within that embryo. The pro-choice faction will say the embryo is nothing more than a clump of cells and nothing about the embryo resembles a human being. Since the fetus can't survive outside the mother, the pro-choice supporters argue that the baby isn't human because it can't live on its own. Yet, if a woman has a crisis in her pregnancy, she'll go to great lengths to save the life of her baby. In one instance, the baby isn't a real human being. And in the other, the baby is very much a human being. These contrary beliefs can be held by the same woman at the same time and by the doctors who are treating her.

I found out later that I was having a conversation with a member of a group that sociologists were calling the "nones." In 2021, Ryan Burger released a book titled *The Nones: Where They Came From, Who They Are and Where They are Going.*[1] Burger, a trained social scientist and an American Baptist pastor, wanted to know how the nonaffiliated population in America had gone from a rounding error to nearly a quarter of the American population.[2] The process of Americans

1. Ryan P. Burger, *The Nones: Where They Came From, Who They Are and Where They Are Going* (Minneapolis: Fortress Press, 2021).
2. Burger, *The Nones*, 4.

walking away from their faith Burger describes in his book has continued to speed up. While he begins by claiming about 25 percent tell us they have no religious engagement with a local congregation, that number is now 60 percent and higher in most parts of the country. While the slide was gradual before the pandemic, the quarantine demanded by most governments meant every church that could, would go online. Families sat at home and watched the services together. If they were single, they had to watch it alone. The impact was devastating in unforeseeable ways. Drug use skyrocketed. Suicides spiked. Mental health issues shot up at an alarming rate.

When we emerged from the pandemic, people didn't come back to church. As I led my church through this challenge, here's what I discovered. About 25 percent of our attendees just left and never came back. They found something else to do on Sunday morning and they never stopped doing it. About 50 percent of our congregation began to split their attendance between being there in person and watching online. The remaining 25 percent kept their regular patterns of attendance. During quarantine, a growing number of people realized that, for them, their religious involvement made no meaningful difference in their lives, and they never came back to church. Our churches were challenged with reaching people we thought we had already reached. These "nones" didn't walk away from their faith after some great crisis of unbelief. They simply decided it didn't matter to them anymore.

I was trained in classical Western philosophy. I grew up on the writings of Augustine and Thomas Aquinas, orthodox

Christian thinkers who started with the Bible and pulled the teachings of the classical Greek philosophers such as Plato, Socrates, and Aristotle into their mental models of the faith. In their writings, Christian theologians hammered out the traditional understanding of the Western Judeo-Christian worldview. Using the philosophical structures of classical Greek philosophy, Christian theologians hammered the teaching of Christianity into a coherent structure. In the outline, Roman numeral I was followed by Roman numeral II. Sub-point A was followed by sub-point B. This theological outline was broken down into ever smaller and smaller pieces. Truth was a statement that corresponded to the reality it was describing. Truth was consistent, coherent, and didn't contradict itself. Truth, according to these theologians, is where the student started. Every other statement was derived from and an implication of the first statement of truth.

Simply put, according to the traditional Christian worldview, truth was established by God in creation. God created the sun and the moon, the stars and the planets, and spun them into their orbits. Somewhere within and scattered all throughout his creation, God folded truth into the reality of our universe. Truth was there to be discovered, revealed by God about himself to be studied, understood, and then lived out in our lives. As humans spread throughout earth, they discovered the truths hidden in creation. Water runs downhill. Objects, when dropped, fall to the ground. Birds fly south when the weather turns cold. People would learn the truth of agriculture, of how seeds, water, and dirt make plants grow to feed their tribes. We would learn the truths of sailing and air travel. We would develop computing and artificial intelligence to discover the vastness and depths of God's creation. In this process, we would learn more about God, ourselves, and how we were to live in the world.

Each time, we would find basic, unchanging statements and then, we would build on these realities to advance our society and culture. These statements were constant. The speed of light didn't change. The force of gravity didn't change. Knowing these dynamics allowed scientists to figure out new realities without ever having seen those realities. Because we knew *this* was true, we knew *that* was true. Because one truth gave us a solid foundation, we assumed we could comprehend other realities. We thought this confidence in the truth of one area of our lives could be transferred to every area of our lives. Life was rational and logical. The truth made sense, and a good life was determined by aligning our lives to the known truth.

Because we believed this was true, evangelism became a logical presentation of one truth leading to another truth that led to an obvious conclusion. When I first started in ministry, most of us were trained in the Billy Graham method of evangelism. We were taught to start off by saying, "The Bible says." This was the starting point. Everyone knew the Bible was the Word of God. Everyone knew the Bible was true. We could argue about how to interpret a certain passage, but no one ever disputed the validity of the Bible. Even people who didn't agree with the Bible's teachings or obey the Bible's dictates thought the Bible was true about God and life. There was almost universal agreement in the truth of Scripture across most of America during this time. Theologians presented their arguments with the confidence of mathematicians. If A was true, then we could know that B was true. The truth of the gospel was a foundational truth, like the speed of light. Something that never changed. The church was sure of this.

The world, however, had its own doubts, and those doubts were growing. Before World War I, most of the world's elites assumed that humanity was on an unstoppable path of human progress. The industrial revolution was changing not only how we made things, but what we could make. The invention of the steam engine, the car, the airplane changed how people lived and what they could afford to buy. Manufacturing and trade made the world richer and richer. When these same inventions, however, were fashioned into the new weapons of war, the world's confidence was broken. The end of World War I brought an end to confidence in the human experiment. We weren't getting better. We were getting worse and nothing, it seems, could be done to stop our downward spiral.

The Jazz Age followed, and people began to believe they should live only for the day because tomorrow wasn't guaranteed to any of us. Death was the great negator of dreams. Too many young men had died in the trenches of Europe. Too many young men returned home from the Great War mangled and hollowed out. The mechanized death of war made people doubt the existence of God, and if they didn't doubt his existence, they certainly doubted his goodness. If there was a God, he wouldn't have allowed the mustard gas to choke the lives of so many young men in the trenches of France and Belgium. The "war to end all wars," as World War I was called, didn't.

Not only did it fail to end all wars, it laid the foundation for World War II that, in turn, led to the conflicts in Korea and Vietnam. While the last two were never officially declared to be wars, the men and women who served in these conflicts will tell you they certainly felt like real wars. The effects on those who served were the same. The push and shove of world politics led to wars in Afghanistan and Iraq. The men and women who returned home from the Middle East made us understand what war did to them.

After World War II, the world got smaller. Trade and commerce were now international. American shoppers were buying goods and services shipped from Japan and China. Workers in America were now competing in a global economy. I remember when the first Japanese cars were first sold in America. To buy a Toyota or a Datsun (now Nissan) was considered un-American. Now, both companies and many more, have factories in the United States. During the seventies and eighties, the economy went up and down, but one thing stayed constant: the top 1 percent of American society controlled more and more of the wealth. For more and more people, there didn't seem to be a way up. Recent economic reports have indicated that for one of the first times in our country's history the rising generation will not do as well financially as their parents.

This has led to a doubting of the American dream and a growing disbelief in America itself. We no longer believed anyone could grow up to be anything they wanted to be. More and more, people were beginning to think the American dream was reserved for only a select few. This growing cynicism challenged the cultural narrative. The narrative, the challengers said, was told mainly by white men for the benefit of white men. Whatever narrative these white men told might be true for them, but it wasn't true for everyone else. If you were a person of color, there were certain opportunities you did not feel were open to you. Their truth wasn't your truth.

Then, Covid-19 hit. We were told this was a worldwide pandemic that would kill millions. Extreme draconian measures would be needed to save humanity. Vaccines were rushed into production. Infected individuals were quarantined. Eventually, our society was shut down altogether. Business offices were closed, and people began working from home. Schools were closed and students were forced to attend classes online. People flooded the internet trying to figure out how to live in the time of pandemic. Sadly, the internet became a dumping ground for misinformation from every side. Some claimed the pandemic was a government hoax designed to gain more and more control over American citizens. Others thought it was a governmental experiment gone wrong, and now the world was threatened with a biological Armageddon. Others said it was a corporate plot to, first, create a crisis, and then, cash in by providing a solution. It didn't help that those in leadership offered messages that were unclear, contradictory, and sometimes just wrong. For instance, we never did figure out the mask question. When was it necessary to wear a mask? When could you not wear a mask? If we did wear a mask, what kind of mask were we supposed to wear?

Whatever trust was left over in our leaders and institutions was lost. We no longer trusted government officials. We didn't trust the experts and a lot of people began to doubt the advice of their own doctors. People began to move from church to church, seeking a church that agreed with their interpretation of the pandemic. Churches struggled to deal with the realities of trying to keep their congregations safe while ministering to their spiritual needs. Neighbors fought neighbors. Families were torn apart. Sometimes it seemed our reaction to the virus was more dangerous than the virus itself.

The book of Judges ends with the sad sentence that every man did what was right in his own eyes. This is where we find ourselves. Everyone is living their own truth. With the shrinking of the world, Americans were exposed to more and more world religions and international thoughts. American evangelicals have found themselves trying to understand Buddhist and Hindu teachings, not in a way to understand the world, but in a way to understand their neighbors.

One of the consequences of this clash of world cultures and individual realities: a lot of major universities stopped requiring standardized testing. Since no student's life experience was standardized, no standardized test could adequately represent a student's preparation for college. Students, depending on their life experiences, may answer differently and, according to their life experience, still correctly do a math problem. Their response to an essay question may vary according to the student's ethnic, economic, and cultural background. Truth, we're told, can't be objectively verified, but must be validated by each person's experience and personal priorities. Truth is no longer objective but is the possession of each individual. Every person has the right to define their reality and truth.

Our culture, in turn, must adapt to every person's expression of their truth.

Now, when the pastor holds the Bible aloft and proclaims, "This is the Word of God," confident the truth of the Bible is a confirmed fact, the congregation isn't so sure. While the preachers state a truth they believe is obvious to everyone, the congregation is weighing the truth claims of the Bible against all the competing truth claims they've heard in the world all week. These claims are numerous and persuasive. The basic American myth of capitalism—that if you only work hard enough, you'll find happiness and success—is no longer universally accepted. Other world religions are presented as life philosophies of love and peace. These other ways of believing are considered just other roads to God. Don't all religions lead to the same place? After all, isn't the only thing that matters is that I'm a good person? Given all these options, Americans do what they do best—they invent something new. More and more Americans pick and choose individual beliefs of various philosophies and religions to create their own blended system of belief.

Americans are practical above all else. Whatever life philosophy one might choose, it must work. In America, we live certain ways because we think it works. That is, if I live my life and do certain things the way they're supposed to be done, I get a nice house, a good job, and a nice retirement. Anything that keeps me from finding my individual happiness is deemed not to work. Many of Jesus's teachings are rejected, not because we believe they're false, but because we don't believe his teachings will work. Turning the other cheek sounds great, but in our dog-eat-dog corporate world, it rarely works. Or so we think.

In the climactic moments of John's Gospel, Jesus has been arrested, tortured, and dragged before the religious leaders of Jerusalem. Lacking the ability to confer the death sentence on Jesus, the Jewish religious leaders sent Jesus before the Roman governor, Pilate. The religious leaders have played their game well. If Pilate releases Jesus, he will be accused of being "soft on crime" and not dealing harshly enough with an enemy of Rome. If the governor gives in and allows Jesus to be executed, he lives with the knowledge of killing an innocent man. Pilate was looking for a way out; if Jesus would just give Pilate something to work with, a legal loophole that would allow Pilate to release Jesus without incurring the wrath of the Jewish leaders or the suspicion of Rome. Pilate asked Jesus if he was a king. Jesus answered that he was a king, but not of this world. When pressed by Pilate, Jesus said he had been born for this, to bear witness to the truth.

That's when Pilate asked the question: "What is truth?" I doubt if anyone present at that moment would have predicted we would still be trying to answer that question. What is truth? If a pollster stood on the street and asked those who walked by, "What is truth?" the pollster would get as many answers as respondents. People would say things such as, "It depends." Depends on what? On a person's culture. What's true in downtown Atlanta might not be true in a village in the Congo. What is true for a senior adult white male might not be true for a Gen Z person of color. Truth, we're told by common wisdom, isn't objective. That is, truth can't stand by its own validity, but must be validated by the experience of the individual. What is true in one moment may not be true in another. What is true for one person doesn't have to be true for another. Truth can be filtered and, thus, altered by personalities, experiences, culture, race, and ethnic background. The answer to Pilate's question is: "It depends."

Another interpretation of "glory" is "weight." We often envision the glory of God as light so brilliant we have to turn our eyes away like Moses on the mountain before God or the apostle Paul confronted by the risen Christ on the Damascus road. Another way to understand the glory of God is to understand it as "heaviness," as in, "putting his weight down." One of the properties of weight is mass, and with mass comes gravity. This means only God has the gravitational mass to hold everything else in our lives in their proper orbit. Without God at the center of our lives, the different aspects of our lives fly out of their assigned orbits, causing confusion and chaos. Only God has the weight of glory to hold everything together in our lives.

The calling of the preacher these days is to place the pulpit in the center of the conversation about truth, reality, meaning, and purpose. As we watch the ministry of Jesus, we see him talking to people at a village well, walking along the road, in people's homes, and along the shore of Lake Galilee. Wherever people were, Jesus was willing to engage those he encountered in the conversation about his Father and his love for them. He didn't always start the conversation, but he was always willing to engage. Like Jesus, we have to begin to understand our pulpit is wherever we are and our congregation is whoever is there in the moment. Our sermons may not have a three-point outline. The sermon may just have one point, depending on the context of the conversation. But we have to understand people are looking for a way to regain control of their out-of-control lives. We're there to remind them only God has the spiritual gravity to hold their lives together, and placing God in the center is the only way the various aspects of their lives find their orbits. Now, how do we do that?

Chapter 2

Strangers in a Strange Land

We're introduced to Joseph when he is seventeen and beginning to come to grips with his own identity. He had dreams of one day ruling the world, but what seventeen-year-old doesn't? Finally, his older brothers had enough of Joseph's ego and his dreams of them one day bowing down to him—so much so that, in a rash of anger, they threw him in a cistern. One group of brothers was going to come back later and rescue Joseph, but before they got back, the other group of brothers sold Joseph into slavery. A wandering group of nomads took Joseph to Egypt, where they sold Joseph again and Joseph eventually ended up as the slave of an Egyptian military commander. Imagine going from being your father's favorite son to a slave in a foreign land over the course of a few days. How would we have responded?

Most of us would have raised quite a disturbance, telling anyone who would listen that we didn't deserve to be a slave and how badly we had been mistreated and wronged. We would scream out how rich and famous our father was and how he would soon be getting a lawyer and sue everybody. That's what I would have done. And because it's what I would have done (and most of you as well), that is the reason there's a story about Joseph and not about me. Joseph's choice was to remain faithful to God despite the circumstances and regardless of whatever situation he had to endure. As the story tells us, Joseph had to endure a great deal. First, he earns the complete trust of his master, Potiphar. The story tells us God was with Joseph and caused everything he touched to prosper. The hand of God was on Joseph so powerfully that even Potiphar noticed. And before long, Potiphar trusted Joseph with all of his household affairs. Joseph, once again, was thriving and everyone around him was doing the same.

The next challenge came when Potiphar's wife tried to seduce Joseph. He refused her advances and told her that her suggestion was a "sin against his master and against God." After all that had happened to Joseph, he still saw himself living under the grace of God. The God of his grandfather, Abraham, and the God of his father, Jacob, was still his God, regardless of the circumstances. Joseph considered his actions to be not only accountable to Potiphar, but to God. When the accusations became known to Potiphar, Potiphar possibly understood the charges against Joseph were false and that's why he put Joseph in prison and didn't kill him. Once again,

Joseph is wrongly accused and mistreated. He was in jail, and it wasn't his fault. So, what did he do?

Joseph did what he had always done. He served well. The warden of prison noticed Joseph and, once again, God was with Joseph and the warden soon placed everything under Joseph's authority. Everything in the prison was better when Joseph was in charge. During his service, Joseph met the cupbearer and the baker for Pharaoh. Each of these men had dreams they couldn't understand. Because of his continued relationship with God, Joseph was given the power to interpret these mysteries. The only thing Joseph asked was to be remembered by the cupbearer when the cupbearer was restored to his position. Of course, the cupbearer either forgot or didn't want to remind Pharaoh that he had been in prison in the first place, so the cupbearer never mentioned Joseph.

Until, that is, Pharaoh had a dream no one could interpret. At long last, the cupbearer comes forward and tells his king about a Hebrew youth who had correctly interpreted dreams while the cupbearer was in prison. Joseph is summoned and not only interprets Pharaoh's dreams but outlines a strategy for Egypt to take advantage of the seven good years to come to be prepared for the seven years of famine that would follow. When Joseph advises Pharaoh to choose a wise leader who can oversee all this, Pharaoh recognizes in Joseph the leader he is looking for. Joseph is appointed to oversee this process, and just like Potiphar's house and the prison before, God's hand is on Joseph and both Pharaoh and Egypt thrive.

Finally, at long last, Joseph's brothers—the same ones who betrayed him—come to Egypt to buy food. Joseph recognizes them and after he puts them through a series of tests, he tells them who he is. The redemption story is complete when Joseph reunites with and is restored to his father and the rest of his family. As a result, two nations are saved from the famine because of Joseph's faithfulness. The children of Abraham live out the famine in Egypt. Once again, God is with Joseph and his people thrive; so much so that the Hebrews' success at the end of Genesis becomes a problem at the beginning of Exodus.

Most of us focus on the misjustice Joseph suffered and how he was able to maintain his integrity despite the hardships forced upon him. What we forget is, through it all, God is working a plan of redemption through Joseph. Joseph is central to this story and his faithfulness to God through it all allows him to stay aligned to the grand narrative of redemption throughout everything he endured. If Joseph had given into his self-pity or anger, if he would have sought revenge against those who wronged him, Joseph would have been disqualified from his availability to God. The story would have had a much different ending.

The story of Daniel is similar. The book of Daniel begins at one of the worst moments in the history of Jerusalem. The city had been destroyed by Nebuchadnezzar's Babylonian armies. The best and brightest of Jerusalem were taken captive and removed back to the Babylonian capital. These captives were trained in the culture, language, and traditions of Babylon and then assigned as bureaucrats for the empire. The Babylonian theory of conquest involved taking the smartest and most talented individuals from a conquered culture, bringing them to the capital city for training and education, then dispersing them throughout the empire as administrators and government officials. The result of Babylon's disbursement of Jewish leadership would have meant the eventual loss of the nation of Israel altogether. Daniel and his friends were some of those brought to Babylon to be trained and educated in the laws and customs of Babylon. The story of Daniel begins with a moment of personal conscience.

Because they were members of the governmental elite, Daniel and his friends ate from the king's table. Babylonian food, of course, wasn't kosher. Daniel made up his mind he wouldn't eat the king's food. This wasn't a matter of personal health. For Daniel, this was an important stand. The Jewish food laws were one of the ways the Jewish people expressed their identities as God's people. Daniel was making a dangerous stand for his faith. When he expressed his dietary concerns to the official in charge of them, the official said no. The king had high expectations for his court officials because they represented the power and wealth of Babylon. Their very appearance of the court officials was testimony it was imperative they appear strong and well fed as they performed their governmental duties. Daniel's decision was putting all that at risk. Not only was Daniel risking his own life, but he was risking all those in charge of him and others. As you can imagine, no one was very supportive of Daniel's idea.

Daniel then suggested they try the diet plan for ten days. After the trial period, the king himself inspected and found Daniel and his friends looked a lot better than all of the other trainees—so much so, everyone was ordered on to Daniel's plan. Nothing succeeds like success. Most of us don't realize the laws of God are given to us to guide us to our best lives. While the law can't make us good people, the law can show us the good way. The law of God is his parental way of saying, "Stay in the yard."

Likewise, Martin Luther King Jr. was abused and wronged by his enemies during the height of the civil rights movement. Like Joseph, he was thrown into prison and falsely accused. King, however, insisted that he and his followers continue to pursue the goals of the civil rights movement in nonviolent response. He refused to give into the world's revenge-centered narrative of "an eye for an eye," which would leave the whole world blind. Martin Luther King Jr. wrote the "Letters from a Birmingham Jail" after being arrested for leading nonviolent protests. The fact that he was unjustly being held in jail gives his writings their power. If King had been duly processed and lawfully arrested and then convicted, he would have been just another troublemaker. As it is, his words changed the course of American history.

So, let's pay attention to these stories. Joseph, Daniel, and Martin Luther King Jr. were known for being different from the people around them. They were ignored, bullied, threatened, and attacked in an effort to get them to conform to cultural expectations. In each case, when tested, what they believed proved better—if not best—for the people around them, even for those who were attacking them. Christians in our culture are different—or they should be. We have different views of marriage, sexuality, morality, love, grace, hope, and well, everything. In conversations, people will often disagree and discount the teachings of Jesus. Our unbelieving friends don't see how the teachings of Jesus actually work in our world. They're seen as weak, idealistic, and even foolish. They will continue to feel this way until they see someone who lives the teachings of Jesus in such a way the person following Christ causes those who are watching to ask questions as they try to figure out how this is even possible.

As Christians, we often forget God is still at work even when we can't see him working. If things aren't going right, if things aren't working out the way we want, we assume that justice is going to be left up to us. We either give up altogether or, worse, try to fix things ourselves. In short, we lose faith, and we lose out on being used by God when the moment is ready. If Joseph had been unfaithful in any of his circumstances, he would have forfeited his place in the greater story of God. Many Christians don't want to stick out. They don't want to be noticed. They choose to blend in, and when they do, they give up all their usefulness to God and his kingdom. Salt that isn't salty isn't good for anything.

Several years ago, I was the teaching pastor of a Tuesday-night young adult worship service called Kairos. I was asked by a group of our young adult leaders to help them get a citywide service started, and I promised to help them. I told them that I didn't have time to lead the service, but I would help them get it up and running. Famous last words. I ended up leading the service for eleven years. During one of the nights, I was teaching about prayer and I could tell by the way they were engaging me and the questions I got from them later that they knew how to pray. They didn't. No one had ever told them how to pray. We had assumed, since most of them had grown up in and around church, that someone would have taught them to pray. We discovered we had to slow things down, way down. We reworked our prayer time so we always included a moment of teaching about prayer, even letting them practice, and then we would let them pray.

We found out they hadn't been taught a lot of things. Most of them didn't have a Bible. They may have had one their parents gave them when they were children, but few of them had a Bible of their own. They would go to the store to buy a Bible but leave the store empty-handed. When I asked them why they didn't buy a Bible, they told me the store had too many Bibles to choose from and they didn't want to buy the wrong one! We ended up having a service where we talked about all the different kinds of translations and the purposes behind each translation. One of the most unforgettable moments of my ministry was talking to them about "their Bible." There was more. No one had taught them about marriage, or careers, or financial management. We had to install an entire life skills curriculum.

Most people are doing as well as they know how to do. We talk about broken families and never stop to fully understand the damage done to the next generation. Children are cut off from their fathers. Sons always learned how to be men from their dads, and now they don't. The crisis of boys in our society is well documented. Girls are having their own problems. Young men get married and try to be husbands having never seen a husband. Young women get married and try to be wives having never seen a wife. They're trying to build families when they've never been part of one.

One of the beautiful truths of grace is when you've lost your own family, God will give you a new one. In small groups, God will give you mothers and fathers, brothers and sisters—all in the faith—that will rebuild what's been lost. We forget most of our neighbors want to live lives of meaning and purpose, they just don't know how.

Maybe somebody should tell them. That's the problem. Everybody has told them. Everyone posts their truth on social media. Everyone who's made a movie and everyone who's recorded a song is now a life coach for our culture. A recent article discussed how a local eatery could no longer keep a certain item on their menu because a certain pop star had revealed in her social media that this food item was one of her favorites. With all these opinions flying through the internet, many people lose themselves in the confusing and sometimes conflicting advice of the so-called "influencers." Many Christian writers, teachers, and preachers have tried to enter this space and have met with some success. These Christian social media platforms are nowhere near the success of the secular and entertainment platforms. Christian influencers just can't be loud enough in this space. How can we as believers get our message out in such a noisy world? The only way we can do it is by being different—by living lives of such qualitative difference our world can't help but notice us. The world is looking for those who can live life well. Sadly, the world doesn't find that when they look at the church.

Since the birth of the church, there has been a constant internal debate on how different the church should be from the world around them. This goes all the way back to the first century, when the apostle Paul had to instruct the Corinthian church concerning the issue of meat sacrificed to idols. In Corinth, the Corinthian church was conflicted on how to respond when offered meat to eat after their pagan hosts had offered the meat to idols. For some believers, there was nothing to this. Idols didn't exist, so whatever was offered to them, including meat, was unchanged and, therefore, good to eat. For other Corinthian Christians, including some new believers who had come out of the pagan lifestyle, the idols were very real. To receive meat offered to another god was to deny the lordship of Jesus Christ. As you can imagine, this caused quite the debate in the early church.

That debate is still ongoing today. How much should a Christian avoid the world and how deeply can they participate in it? At what point does the Christian, like a hermit, disconnect so completely from the world that they no longer have any influence on the world at all? On the other hand, when is the Christian so immersed in the culture around them that they are no longer distinct from the culture around them and, again, have no influence at all? The Amish have taken one approach. Progressive Christians have taken another. The Amish have chosen to live a simple life with very little influence or even interaction with the world around them. They are known to be great craftsmen, but don't use any power tools. The use of electricity is considered worldly.

At the other extreme would be the growing number of bourbon and cigar Bible studies men are involved in around the country. Men, drawn together by their love of premium cigars and quality whiskeys, get together in homes, back porches, and cigar shops to open their Bibles and talk about themselves, their families, and their faith. I would hate to think what my little mill-village church would think about smokes and brews for Jesus. Yet, this is a very sincere and, some would say, effective method of outreach and discipleship. As you can tell, this debate is still going on.

Here's where the rubber meets the road. Every church will tell their new pastor they want a pastor just like them. They don't. They will tell you that they want you to be one of the guys, but they don't. They'll tell you to loosen up and enjoy yourself and all will be well . . . until, of course, you have to make a stand. When you stand up and tell the church this is what God says and this is what God expects, the church will shrug and say, "Why should we listen to you? You're just like us."

The world isn't mad at the church for being different. The world is mad at the church for not being different enough. For a long time, we were told there was no statistical difference between Christians and non-Christians when it came to addiction, divorce, pornography, and other issues of morality. We found out those statistics aren't exactly true. Depending on how we define the word *Christian* makes a lot of difference in how we understand the numbers. Those we would consider theologically conservative don't use porn or get divorced at the same rates. Here's the problem: the world doesn't know the difference. Few people would be able to recognize the different brands of Christianity. Not only do they not know, they don't care. For the world outside the church, they don't see a difference. Recent moral failures of high-profile ministers have only added to the world's growing cynicism toward the church. Add this to the ongoing child abuse scandals among various denominations and a lot of people have concluded its safer to avoid church altogether.

Here's what I tell young pastors: congregations watch before they listen. They watch the way you walk around the sanctuary. They watch how you greet members. They watch how you react when your spouse walks up to you. They watch how you respond to your children. With each interaction, your congregation and the community around them are deciding if you're the kind of preacher they can trust. Is there something in your life that would give your words credibility? On the other hand, is there something that they see in your walk that would cause them to not listen to your sermon? Do your actions and your words align? In short, does your life have integrity? Remember, your congregation and community are the most marketed to generations in history. Each week they are overrun by ads, pop ups, commercials, emails, and mailers. They have become pretty good at sifting hype from the truth.

In those moments, when we decide we don't want to be different from the world around us, we give up the very thing the world needs from us. They need to see someone live a different life. They need to see there's another way to live. Jesus brings us a better way to live. Jesus teaches us how to be better husbands, to be better wives, and to be better parents. He teaches us how to deal with a painful or disappointing past. He teaches us how to forgive when we've been wronged and find healing in the midst of all the hurt. Paul tells the Corinthians their emphasis on the spiritual gifts is well and good, but he will teach them a better way, and what follows is one of the most quoted passages in all the Bible, 1 Corinthians 13.

Christians do have a better way. We have the wisdom of God in Christ Jesus teaching us who we are and what in life matters. We have his Spirit in us, allowing us to forgive each other and live in grace with each other. Most of our neighbors, congregations included, don't believe it because they've never seen it.

There's never a time that the preacher isn't preaching. Our calling isn't to a job or a career. It's a calling to a life. Our spoken sermons are just one part of our preaching. It may be the only sermon our people hear, but it's not the only one they're watching.

We are, indeed, living in a strange time and place. The nation we know now is very different from the nation in which we were raised. As challenging as living in these times might be, we're no different than Daniel or Joseph or any of the saints before us. They had to find their way in a strange land, and we must do the same. Our world won't believe any sermon they hear until they see it first.

Chapter 3

The Challenge of First Sermons

I remember my first sermon. It was awful. I had just told my little home church I felt called to the ministry, and the membership, most of whom I had known all my short life, rallied around me to confirm God's hand on my life. They, unknown to me, had recognized God's calling on my life long before I did. In those days, going into the ministry meant you were going to be a preacher. There was no understanding of going into counseling or student work. If you were called, you were going to preach. Some would become missionaries, but everyone was going to be a preacher.

So, if you were going to preach, you might as well get started. I was scheduled to preach on a Sunday night in about two weeks. No one told me about how to write a sermon or how I needed to structure my sermon. No one told me about the importance of an attention-grabbing introduction. No one told me how to craft the sermon, about how one point should be connected to the next point and how the sermon should conclude with a strong call to action. No one told me anything except to just get up there and preach.

And I didn't ask. I was called to preach and if I was called to preach, I shouldn't have to worry about what I would say when I stood up in front of my church. Jesus promised that to his followers. It was right there in the Bible. The night came and, wearing my best suit, I stood up to preach. Whatever inspiration I was supposed to feel never showed up. Whatever emotional conviction was supposed to well up in me to preach a sermon that would change the world never came. I preached for about five minutes and then prayed as I concluded. I didn't actually conclude anything. I just ran out of things to say, and I stopped. Praying was the only thing I knew to do to make the evening stop. I was so humiliated and embarrassed I didn't preach again for years. But my home church never gave up on me. God bless little churches that will happily sit through some of the worst sermons ever preached and still love the preacher anyway.

Every preacher harbors the secret fantasy that preaching must have been easier to preach at some other time. There must have been a time when congregations were more open and eager to hear the Word. There had to be moments when a community would gather in prayerful anticipation to what the preacher would have to say, when people would hang on to every word that flowed from the preacher's mouth. We read about preachers in the First Great Awakening preaching sermons that lasted for over two hours, and we marvel at what that must have been like. That was also before the internet and all the other modern inventions of distraction. People didn't have much else to do except go to church. There were just as many social reasons for attending church as there were spiritual reasons.

The fact is preaching has always been hard. People have fickle attention spans. Sometimes people are difficult to read and, therefore, it's hard to gauge how to direct the sermon. Does the congregation have a theological background? If so, how deep is that background? Even if the congregation has a very shallow understanding of the Christian God, do they have a lot of other spiritual knowledge or just bad theology? How much of their thinking has to be deconstructed before a positive case for the gospel can be built? All of this and much more has to be ascertained by the preacher before the first word is ever preached. Preaching has always been and continues to be a very difficult and complicated process.

Perhaps it would have been different if we had been on the shores of the Sea of Galilee when Jesus walked by. Hearing him call our name would make all the difference for our preaching. We believe we would have followed him without hesitation or qualification. We would have been model disciples. We would have hung on every word and understood every teaching. We would have recognized the dimensions of every parable. Of course, this is all in our imagination.

As it is, we're trying to follow Jesus in a time when we can't see him. We can know him, but we can't see him. Our world is complicated and openly hostile to the faith. We could have preached like Paul. We could have preached like Peter.

It had to be easier preaching in the early days of Christianity. Being there would have been proclaiming a message as it was happening. How hard could that be? A closer reading of the text tells us that preaching those first sermons may have been more difficult than we care to acknowledge.

The Roman Empire spread from Spain to the Middle East, across northern Africa and almost all of Europe. While the Romans had a lenient policy toward local religions and gods, no one could question the supremacy of the emperor's cult. Anything, or anyone, that threatened the worship of the emperor was considered treasonous and dealt with accordingly. When Peter proclaimed the risen Christ, he directly challenged the authority of Rome. Besides that, Jerusalem was the center of the Jewish faith. The high priest was a recognized authority in Jewish life. Peter's sermon was a direct challenge to the Jewish authorities. While all the Jews expected a Messiah to come, no one who heard Peter's sermon was willing to name Jesus as the Promised One. Not only did Peter have the improbable message of Christ being raised from the dead, he preached his Pentecost sermon directly in the face of two worldviews (Roman and Jewish) that were violently opposed to the gospel.

We have at least two instances when the apostle Paul was challenged to preach to hostile audiences. The first was in Athens, when he was invited to present his gospel message to a gathering of philosophers and teachers. Paul famously begins his sermon by acknowledging the deep religiosity of his listeners. He points out the great statues to the gods that adorned the great city of Athens and then drew the attention of the Athenians to a statue of the unknown god. Paul, seizing on the opportunity, preached the gospel of Jesus. While some objected to his teaching on the resurrection, others were inclined to discuss his message more.

Paul's strategy has been discussed among Christian leaders almost since he preached the message. Some see it as a brilliant way to connect to a point of concern of his listeners. After all, while the Athenians were sure their pantheon of gods covered everyone, they were at least open to the possibility that they may have missed one. Paul seized on that fear and used it as the opening for his sermon. Others see it as a mistake. According to this view, Paul compromised the uniqueness of the gospel in an effort to make it more acceptable to his listeners. They point to his emphasis to the Corinthians of preaching Christ and him crucified as a sign of Paul's remorse for his failed strategy in Athens. Personally, I appreciate Paul's strategy. While it may not have had the impact he desired (no sermon does, for that matter), he did create an environment for a second conversation. Any sermon that ends with your hearers wanting to hear more is a good sermon.

The second sermon from Paul was his defense before Agrippa at the end of Acts. I think we read this passage too fast. We need to let the circumstances of this sermon settle down within us before we read the text. Remember, Paul is on trial for his life. He's been in and out of prison for preaching the gospel. And now, Agrippa gives Paul a chance to speak for himself. Paul has a chance to clear his name against the trumped-up charges being brought against him. If he positioned his argument correctly, Paul could walk out a free man.

What does Paul do? He preaches a sermon. Beginning with his own testimony, Paul boldly proclaims the risen Christ, even giving an invitation for Agrippa to believe himself. Needless to say, Paul didn't go free. Yet, for Paul, the issue was never about his freedom. He was a slave to the gospel, and if his being in prison served the cause of the gospel, Paul would live with that. He writes in Philippians 1:12–14:

> Now I want you to know, brethren, that my circumstances have turned out for the greater progress of the gospel, so that my imprisonment in the cause of Christ has become well known throughout the whole praetorian guard and to everyone else, and that most of the brethren, trusting in the Lord because of my imprisonment, have far more courage to speak the word of God without fear. (NASB1995)

The New Testament itself gives us models on how to preach in an unbelieving, or worse, uncaring world. Let's look at these well-known New Testament sermons and see if we can discern a pattern. Peter in Jerusalem and Paul in Athens use similar approaches. For instance, both Peter and Paul start with where their hearers are. Paul addresses the idols around the city and Peter begins by quoting the Old Testament prophets. In both cases, Peter and Paul begin their sermons at points connecting their hearers with their own experience. Both preachers seem to be saying to their hearers, "Both you and I know these things to be true about your lives." Athens is a very religious city and the Athenians themselves admit they may have left a god or two out of the pantheon. For a spokesman to say he's been sent on behalf of the unknown God doesn't totally surprise the Athenians. Paul has quickly established a platform from which to address his audience with some level of authority. Peter begins by reminding the gathering crowd in Jerusalem that God had promised this time would come when old men dreamed dreams and young men prophesied. That these dreams and prophecies were now coming to pass shouldn't surprise Jerusalem. Peter's and Paul's sermons were already gaining credibility because the preachers had set their sermon within the conversational context of their listeners.

Here's our first point: when preaching in an unbelieving culture, the preacher has to connect the sermon to the conversations and concerns our listeners are already having. Too many times, preachers will begin an evangelistic sermon or conversation without ever establishing any points of agreement. The gospel will be lost in a word salad of religious jargon, and the listener will never understand why they should be concerned. Religious words and phrases such as *lost* and *born again* have profound and deep meanings. It's part of our culture and faith language. Yet, to most of our friends and neighbors, the terms have at best no meaning and at worst, they're used only in jokes of secular comedy. How would we try and communicate these issues if we had to speak a different language? That's the point. We are having to preach in a different language and in a different culture, and one of the best ways to do that is to remind them this is a story they've been telling all along and the gospel message answers some of their deepest concerns.

Now, to the second point: connect the gospel message to where they already are. One of the mistakes we make is assuming the sermon is a monologue. In reality, the best sermons are dialogues, whether implied or actual. In this conversation, we hear the stories of our congregations and neighbors. We hear stories of failure and heartache, of brokenness and regret. We hear stories of success, and then ultimate disappointment when the newfound success brings only temporary happiness, if any at all. This is the story of the human condition. Every human being knows the lyrics to this song, and this is one of the reasons the gospel rings true in the first place. For sure, the gospel tells us the truth about God, but it also tells us the truth about ourselves. Sure, we may use different words to describe our plight, but everyone in the room will recognize the reality of the plight being described. This is us. This is our lives. This is the mess we're in, and we can't fix it.

"Woe is me," Isaiah cries out. "I am a man of unclean lips and live among a people of unclean lips" (Isa. 6:5). Not only does Isaiah realize his life is a mess and, therefore, has no chance before God, everyone he knows is messed up and has no chance before God. Not only are we not going to make it, but we also don't know anyone who *is* going to make it. Does our sermon have a point where we help our listeners understand this is what it means to be human? This is the reality we all know. Even Jesus, hanging on the cross, experiences our existential loneliness and despair. The preacher has a chance if the listener is thinking, "Yes, this is how I am. Yes, this preacher understands what it's like to be me." If the preacher can accurately communicate that they understand what the congregation is going through, if we can start from that point of connection, perhaps they will listen when we move to the next step.

And what is that next step? God understands the human condition. Through Christ, God has experienced the human reality himself and, knowing we can't get to him, God has come to us. This is where the sermon moves to God's story. This is the part of the story where we get to talk about a God who created everything and wants a relationship with all he's created. So much so, he sent his Son to pay our penalty. There's always a penalty isn't there? If we know anything in our world, we know our rebellion has demanded a devastating cost. Think about it. Our greed has led to global warming. Our idolatry has demanded the sacrifices of our children and our families. Generations have been broken by addictions and despite spending millions of dollars in education and prevention, we lose young people by the thousands. Jesus has paid this price with his own life, in his own death. We don't have to keep suffering like this. We can be free not only of the penalties, but of the consequences of our mistakes.

And that's not all. Not only has God provided a covering for our pasts, but he's also made a way for a new future. There is a better way to live. Not only is there a better way to live, but there's also a better way to live the life you've always wanted. We want to have meaning and purpose in our lives. We want to know we lived for something, that our lives counted for something. The gospel message is we were created on purpose for a purpose. How better to know that purpose than in conversation with the One who created us? We are more than the accidental collision of carbon and protein. There is a reason to our living, a kingdom meaning within our lives. This is the second part of the good news we preach.

Too many sermons focus so intently on justification, the forgiveness of our sins, and the future coming of Christ, our glorification, that we overlook the good news of sanctification, the daily process of becoming more and more like Christ. In our prayers and Bible study, in our worship and obedience, we learn more and more about how Jesus wants us to live our lives. We learn to forgive. We learn to speak with kindness and graciousness. We learn to give up worry. In short, we begin to experience life in the Spirit. We receive in our own lives the gifts of the Spirit—love, joy, peace, patience, kindness, goodness, faithfulness, gentleness, and self-control.

The buzz word in our culture is *discipline*. Every business section in every bookstore is filled with books about self-discipline. We're told by our secular culture that our success in life is dependent upon our ability to discipline our lives to achieve our goals. If we can just keep focused and on task, we can lose weight, increase our personal productivity, and find the lives of our dreams. That doesn't happen, does it? First, we live in a world filled with distractions. As anyone who's tried to lose weight can confirm, staying focused and willful for an entire day is exhausting and, ultimately, unworkable. The most successful of us create systems that support our choices and goals. For instance, if we want to lose weight, we schedule our workouts with a buddy and we only have healthy food in our homes. Let me tell you from personal experience, a cookie in the house will be one that we end up eating.

The saints among us have been teaching us this for generations. They create spiritual habits. They read their Bibles, write in their journals, and pray at the same time every day. They go to church at the same time every week and, yes, some of my friends go to church every day. As one of my friends told me, "I need to check in with the boss every day. If I don't, I'll forget who's the boss." One of the most important processes of discipleship is to help the new believer establish new habits. This is one of the most important, yet overlooked, parts of helping new believers mature in their faith. One of the most common mistakes of young believers is not establishing new habits. New believers need to start hanging out with new friends and doing different things on Sunday. It's the way the teachings of Christ become embedded into the lives of his followers.

Everyone these days seems to have a coach. Chief executives have coaches. Athletes have all kinds of coaches—strength, nutrition, and skill coaches who develop the athlete's abilities to the highest levels of excellence. There are coaches for hobbies and games of all kinds. There are marriage coaches and career coaches. But there's one thing everyone looks for in a coach. Has the coach done what the one seeking training wants to do? Nothing will disqualify a coach faster than never having done what they're coaching about.

And life coaches. Here's where our conversations get interesting. Most of our friends and neighbors want to do better in living their lives. They just don't know how. As I said earlier, we have husbands who are trying to be husbands who have never seen a good husband and wives trying to be wives when they have never seen a good wife. Parents, who weren't raised by good parents, are trying to be good parents. Young adults who are beginning their lives, but don't know how to get started. When they look around to see who can help them, they'll be looking for those who are living the lives they want to live. This is when we pray our neighbors see Christians.

Can we help them, they will ask, to find meaning in their life? Can we help them find purpose? Can we help them find out who they are and why they are here in the first place? Can they be a good father when they don't have a good father? Can they break the cycles of the past—cycles that have caused so much pain in their own lives? Are they doomed to repeat the past in their own futures?

And this is where you'll preach your first sermon. No, it probably won't be behind a pulpit in a grand cathedral. More than likely, it'll be in a booth at your favorite coffee shop or a favorite chair in your own living room, but this will be where you preach your first sermon. How will you begin? How will you make your points? Don't panic. Remember, we've been doing this a very long time. Use the examples of Peter and Paul to guide you in your moment. Tell your own story. Tell the story of Jesus. Ground the stories in God's great story of salvation and redemption. Don't worry if the conversion continues until another time. Jesus and Nicodemus probably had more than one conversation. Paul needed three years in the wilderness to figure it all out. Peter needed daily instruction from Jesus for three years to get it all together in his head and heart. Don't be surprised if it takes more than one conversation. Do what you can. Say what you can and trust God with the rest.

Chapter 4

It May Take a Miracle

In the mid-nineties, I urged the missions ministry of our church to find an AIDS ministry with which we could partner. Due to the political climate of the Nashville area, I told them that no one will take us seriously unless we're engaged with the pandemic of AIDS. Since Brentwood is a suburb of Nashville, I was thinking the team would come back with a ministry located in the downtown area of the city. To my surprise, they brought back a recommendation for our church to partner with a church in Cape Town, South Africa. A church? On the other side of the world? What could they be doing in South Africa to impact AIDS?

I should have waited to ask my question until after I met John Thomas.

Let me introduce you to John Thomas. John grew up in South Africa during the rising conflicts over apartheid. He became pastor of the Fish Hoek Baptist Church in Cape Town and began to do what Baptist preachers do. He started trying to grow his church and even started a building program. When I visited the church, I could see where the construction stopped when John came to church with a burden about what was going on across the street. Across the street was an illegal settlement that became the township of Masiphumelele. While the poverty was beyond what most of us can imagine, the real danger was the rampant spread of AIDS in the settlement. Unable to get these images out of his heart, John led his church to abandon their building program and respond to the medical and social epidemic across the street. Fish Hoek Baptist Church began Living Hope, a ministry responding to the AIDS crisis in the townships around their church.

What began as a hospice and medical education ministry soon developed into a center for family counseling, family health, job training, medical personnel training, and of course, church planting. Soon our church leaders were on a plane to get to know John and review his ministry plan. We have never been the same from those initial conversations. Over the following years, John and I would become close friends, and our churches would connect deeply as the Living Hope ministry continued to develop more and more responses to the disease and related consequences on the settlements of South Africa and neighboring countries as the ministry continued to expand.

Let me give you some of the background. John became the pastor of Fish Hoek Baptist Church in 1987. South Africa was still under apartheid at the time. John and his church, however, became concerned about several people who were camping illegally across the road not far from the church.

When visiting with John, I asked him what had prompted his efforts that began the ministry. "Matthew 25 scared me to death," he said. "I was scared I would one day stand before Jesus and he would say, 'John, you did pretty well with that little group of Baptists I gave you, but what about the thousands of people who were just across the street?'"

Under John's leadership, his church started a black church in the middle of the camp. Remember, this was the apartheid era. Working within the black townships was very controversial and bold for a white Baptist church. When the settlements were legalized, the people of the township insisted their new church be placed in the center of the camp to symbolize the church's faithfulness to the settlement before and during apartheid. While John was working with the pastor and the church's leadership in the middle of Masiphumelele (the settlement's new name), John became aware of what AIDS was doing to the township.

The first figure John heard was 44 percent. Forty-four percent of the people in the township had AIDS. While that number was later proven to be too high (the actual rate was 17%), the stark reality of what was going on across the street from his church haunted John. Remember, at the time there was no treatment or cure for AIDS. Due to the extreme poverty of the area, basic hygiene and comfort measures were all lacking. Without a basic understanding of the disease, AIDS was growing at an alarming rate. Children were orphaned, and entire families were killed by the pandemic. Stories of grief never seemed to end. John was so overcome he didn't know where to start. He determined that, however, with God's help, he would do something. So, he started. Not everyone was thrilled. John had to overcome opposition within the leadership of his own church. Governmental officials weren't supportive, and the residents of the settlement were suspicious. John even had to confront local witch doctors who were telling infected men that having sex with young virgins would cure them.

John's first step was a simple one. In 1999, John organized a medical team led by Professor Barbara Robertson, a nursing professor at a nearby university. Her team began HIV and AIDS outreach work in Masi through informal health care and support. The visiting nurses would move from house to house in the settlement, treating victims, working with families, and holding impromptu AIDS educational seminars with the community. This was followed up by church members who would visit and pray with those who were sick and their families. Small Bible studies sprung up. Friendships connected as neighbor loved neighbor. As their efforts grew, the need for a stand-alone center, separate from the church, became urgent. In July 2000, John and the church were able to acquire property in an area opposite the township. A trust was established called the Fish Hoek Baptist Church Community Trust. Focused on preaching the gospel, the center expanded from the prevention, care, and treatment of HIV and AIDS to community development through education and health-related programs, as well as other things. The center eventually grew to fifty-one various programs in health care, substance abuse recovery, life skills, family strengthening, and agricultural training.

To everyone's surprise, the church's ministry was successful. Patients went from acute to chronic (yes, that's an improvement). They got well enough to go home. With this, Living Hope was granted more and more opportunities such as moving from emphasizing hospice work to job training. The hospital developed a hospice ministry early on, but that was only the beginning. The ministry began to develop preventive ministries such as sex education courses that were eventually taught in every nearby school. Our church became a committed partner with John Thomas and Living Hope. We helped them design a work training program the patients could take back to their villages. Patients were taught to grow vegetables in hydroponic tubs filled with tilapia. The fish were sold to local restaurants and the vegetables were sold at local markets.

Soon the world began to recognize the work of Living Hope, and people came from all over the world to see their success. The work of Living Hope was even noticed by President George W. Bush. He supported the work by extending a presidential grant to Living Hope. John was invited to speak around the world at health and church conferences. Inadvertently, John Thomas had become a recognized expert in community health, AIDS treatment, psychological and social support of communities and families, and the biblical command of Jesus to reach out to the "least of these."

When John preaches, people listen. As far as the techniques of preaching go, however, John's average. He doesn't have a big voice or a large presence in the pulpit. His explanation of his chosen text is simple. Most of the time when he preaches, he'll preach directly from Matthew 25 or some related text. But when he closes his sermon and calls for a response, the congregation will move. There will be those who come to follow Christ, but more will come forward to go back to South Africa with John. They want to be part of the work Living Hope is doing. For them, what John Thomas and Living Hope is doing is a mission worthy of their lives.

Working with John taught me many things. The first lesson I learned was how eager congregations were to do hard things; not only do hard things, but take on impossible things like the AIDS pandemic. The people within our congregations do remarkable and amazing things every week. They secure business deals, lead companies, and write books. They solve city problems and run local governments. They raise families and volunteer in ways that make everything in our cities and towns work. They are people of amazing talents and abilities, but these abilities are never engaged by our churches. For most church leaders, a good member attends often and gives regularly. But the hard truth is that most of our people are bored. We never call them to do great things. Their commitment to Christ, for us anyway, is shown by their weekly attendance. Our members want to do more. Our world needs our churches to do more.

They should do more. Why? Because the world never deals with the root problem that causes all of these other problems. Poverty, addiction, greed, war, and all the rest are symptoms of the fallenness of humanity. Giving a homeless person a house doesn't solve the problem of homelessness. The problems that caused the homelessness need to be addressed. Getting an addict to stop using their drug of choice is only the beginning of the process, not the end. Once the cycle of use has been interrupted, the hard part of piecing back together a broken life that allowed the addiction to begin in the first place has to be addressed. This usually requires a complete restructuring of the ways the person thinks, feels, and decides. Healing requires a total reworking of the heart, mind, and spirit. Alcoholics Anonymous calls a person who is no longer drinking but who hasn't done the hard work of dealing with the issues that drove their addiction a "dry drunk." They still carry the pain that drove them to begin drinking, but they just aren't drinking right now.

The total healing of the person can only be done by the gospel. Only the gospel can heal the deep wounds within all of us. Once those wounds are healed by the grace of Christ, then healing throughout that person's life will follow—relationally, spiritually, emotionally, and physically. The healing the world needs is holistic healing, not just symptomatic. This requires a full and deep preaching of the gospel message.

This isn't new. This goes back to the early history of the church. From the beginning, Christians saw themselves as the protectors of the weak and outcasts of society. Both the Greek and Roman cultures practiced infant abandonment. Parents who thought their children were inferior or weak for whatever reason would leave their infants in the forest and wilderness places outside the city to be claimed by nature, whether it be wild animals or exposure. The early Christians would save these babies, adopt them, and raise them as their own. During the plague, Christians were known for their care of the sick and dying. Throughout history, Christians have started schools, hospitals, orphanages, rehab centers for addictions, and hospice care for the dying. Mother Teresa went to India to care for the dying lepers of Mumbai. Because she was doing something no one wanted to do, no one in the city bothered her. Yet, because she did something so humane and unquestionably good, she was given a worldwide platform. She was routinely invited to speak to leaders and influencers around the world.

This is what I call the "Mother Teresa Rule": Go where no one wants to go and do what no one wants to do. The church should prayerfully take on the impossible problems of their communities, and when they do, the communities will give them a platform and an audience for the preaching of the gospel. The community ministry and the preaching aren't two different things. They are simply two different ways of doing the same thing. One is through action that leads to conversation and the other is conversation that leads to action. In our postmodern world, the two cannot be separated. Talk without action and people stop listening. Action without conversation means the world never understands the true meaning of the action. The church must be willing and able to do both. We've done this in the past and we can do it again. What's more, we have the necessity of doing it again. Our world is so broken. We've exhausted all our human efforts, and nothing has worked. Our humanity is so broken that the solutions we choose today become the problems we have to solve tomorrow.

In the New Testament, Jesus will often perform a miracle and then begin to teach the gathered crowds. Our world is looking for a similar miracle, but their expectation of miracles is a lot smaller than we would expect. Our world is so dark and depressing, anything that breaks the normal conversation of the day is considered a miracle. Whenever we talk about miracles, we usually think about diseases being healed and the dead being raised back to life. Our world isn't nearly as demanding. Life has become so broken and painful that little things such as getting to work without getting hung up in traffic is considered a small miracle. Some of that is an abuse of the language. Everything is "awesome," "incredible," and yes, "miraculous." We use the words so often that we aren't even sure what they mean anymore. Nowadays, people use these words to describe anything out of the ordinary.

For most people, the ordinary is, well, disappointing. For one of the first times in American history, the rising generation isn't expected to do better than their parents. The American dream is in doubt. People aren't sure if life is working for them. We're hearing terms such as "quiet quitting." People are showing up for work, but they aren't working. They're doing enough to get by, but they're no longer going the extra mile or pushing for a promotion. They're doing just enough. Most people are beginning to think there's nothing in it for them. The extra effort just isn't worth it. Thousands of men in the prime working years of their lives have dropped out of the workforce. In survey after survey, people don't believe the country is headed in the right direction.

The church can no longer simply seek refuge within the four walls of the sanctuary and wait for Jesus to return. The world needs the pastoral ministry of the church. The gospel of Jesus requires it. Jesus told the story of the Good Samaritan for a reason. Who are the followers of Christ? Christians are the ones who stop and help. If you're a follower of Christ and want to know God's will for your life, look and find the point of need closest to you. For our gospel to be heard, the church must get back into the miracle business.

I want to be clear. I'm not talking about the social gospel. For generations, evangelicals have debated the false issue of evangelism and community ministry. The criticism against the social gospel is that the church spends too much effort on the physical needs of the community and then assumes the good deeds would speak for themselves. Rarely does it work out that way. People assume the ministry is just another nonprofit doing good deeds. Onlookers never see the deeper meaning of the work. They would think kindness was all there was to it. The world needs to hear the rest of the story.

How do we do this? By thinking like missionaries. How would a missionary work in our community? They would look for a place to do good and then share the gospel from there. We can do the same. For example, every church has a school nearby. What if every church adopted the local school nearest them? What if they walked over to the school and said, "We have no agenda. We're here to help."? What if the church provided needed supplies for the teachers and tutors for every child that needed one?

Our campuses were required to engage with a local school. The stories are amazing and heartbreaking, all at the same time. One church invited the teachers of a nearby school to a back-to-school luncheon. They shared lunch and a musical program (in Nashville, everything has music). As they got up to leave, they were told to pick up the plastic bin with their name on it and inside they would find all the school supplies they had requested for the new school year.

Another church tells the story of a young mother who came into the church offices and was very upset. Her son was graduating elementary school and, in the fall, would start at a new middle school. She was upset because she thought it meant her son would lose his mentor, who was a member of our local congregation. When we explained that his mentor was a gift from our church to the school and wasn't a school employee, she couldn't believe what she was hearing. Her son's mentor could stay with her son through middle school. Being a mentor was part of his service to Christ. He didn't work for the school board. He would work with her son as long as he was needed.

Tutors, food pantries, clinics, and rehab centers—the opportunities are endless, and these are things the church has done for years. The church responded to the plague in the Middle Ages by burying the dead and caring for the sick. In the process, we started hospitals. Alcoholics Anonymous had its beginning in the church. Samuel Shoemaker, an Episcopal priest, worked with Bill Wilson (known as Bill W.) to design the twelve-steps program. The Southern Baptist Convention is nationally known for its disaster relief ministries. Places like New Orleans, Houston, and the northeast United States know well the quality of the service these men and women provide. Even the public school systems, colleges and universities, and many of the institutions we take for granted in our culture were started in the church. It's time we reclaimed our heritage of healing and hope.

What does a church have to do to get started? Nothing. I'm serious. Nothing. The worst thing that can happen is for a local church to get convicted about reaching its community, throw a bunch of programs at the so-called problems, and spend a lot of money and time on a perceived problem. I say perceived problems because the issues that plague our cities and towns are complicated and multifaceted. For instance, when we try to address homelessness, we quickly encounter the connected issues of addiction and mental illness. To put someone in a house without addressing the other related issues doesn't solve the problem. Even feeding the homeless, while necessary and the Christian thing to do, is only a momentary answer to this crisis. The person will just be hungry again tomorrow and the problems will continue.

So, how does a church find its place to engage? By prayerfully seeking the Spirit's guidance together. Do you remember all the times in the New Testament when believers came together, prayed, and made a decision that "seemed good to them." The Council of Jerusalem in Acts 15 is one of those times. Prayer is vital to community ministry. Without prayer, any effort by the church is doomed to failure. The church isn't looking to provide another social service, but to make an impact for the kingdom of God. The question isn't, "Where can we help?" but, "What can we do that best shows the kingdom of God in action?" After all, the church prays, "On earth as it is in heaven." This is one of those moments where the future kingdom leaks into our present reality.

While we don't need to be naive about the seriousness of these issues, we shouldn't be frightened into inaction. While we can't do everything, we can do something. So, where do we start? We begin by walking around our neighborhood and prayerfully searching for ways our churches can make a difference. Where does our community need us to engage? Is it the local school? Is there a local park that needs to be cleaned up? Can the church set up a food pantry? Clothes closet? Counseling center? Don't worry if what you come up with has never been done before. Your answer will be as unique as your congregation and community. There's no one size fits all.

Next, do something. What we do doesn't have to be earth-shattering, but we must start. Great things are often the result of small beginnings. Open your church to the homeless during the cold winter nights. Provide blankets to those who are living on the streets. Find a piece of neglected property, buy it, and build low-income housing. Open a soup kitchen. Offer free haircuts. Teach classes so our new friends can obtain a GED. Don't worry that we can't do all we want to do. Don't worry that we can't do all we know we should do. The most important thing to do is to start. When we are faithful to show up with whatever we have at the moment, with whatever understanding we have in the moment, Jesus is faithful to amplify our efforts with his grace and power. There's a reason the church has been telling the story of Jesus feeding five thousand people for all these years. We've seen it happen all the time. We show up in obedience and faith, bringing our few fish and loaves, and Jesus multiplies the impact. For this to happen, however, more churches are going to have to start showing up.

When we start showing up, people will begin to ask questions. People will want to know why we're doing what we're doing. That's when we get to tell them about the love of Jesus. We get to say Jesus tells us to love our neighbors and we thought this would be a good way to show this. We get to tell our new friends about a love of Jesus so abundant it overflows from our lives into the lives of others. We get to tell them of a love so profound it won't let us sit quietly when we see others suffering. We get to tell them of a Savior who identifies so completely with the outcasts that anything we do for them we have done for him. When one of our campuses offered their neighbors free help to file their income taxes, they went door to door to tell the neighbors about the free assistance. One neighbor opened the door, listened to the church's invitation, and said he was an accountant and would love to help. He also mentioned he was an atheist, but since the atheists weren't doing anything, did we mind if he came and helped. No, we said, we didn't mind, and the gospel conversation started before the event did!

We found this happening all the time. Everyone would know about the problem, the community would say, but no one had done anything about it. When the church showed up and started doing even the smallest things, the neighbors would not only appreciate the efforts of the church but join the church in serving the community. The acts of love were contagious. People were intrigued to know more about the neighborhood church that was setting up the food pantry, clothes closet, GED classes, and job fairs. It didn't have to be much, but it had to be something. Some action that recognized the humanity of the neighbors. Some action that revealed the love of God, a love that refuses to sit idly by when nearby friends hurt. A love that acts. I guess love is its own miracle. In our time of desperation and despair, it doesn't take the kind of miracles we so often talk about. Any act of love will do.

All of us know a great sermon needs great illustrations, a story that makes the sermon unforgettable. It's one thing to say to our congregations, "Jesus loves our neighbors." Everyone would agree with that. What makes it unforgettable is a story like John Thomas and Living Hope. What would make the sermon even more memorable is a story of our own churches loving our own neighbors. Every church needs to find and start its own Living Hope.

Chapter 5

What We've Seen and Heard

Nashville is the worst place in the world for name-dropping. Whenever you're in any conversation someone in the group will mention they know (fill in the blank with your favorite musical superstar). The group, suspicious, will ask some questions: "When did you meet them?" "What are they like?" Upon this intense grilling by their friends, the person will finally admit they don't actually know the superstar but saw them at a local restaurant. Sadly, most people who claim to be followers of Christ are only name-droppers. They may have heard about Jesus when they were children going to church with their parents. They may have had a spiritual encounter, a fleeting moment when they sensed an unnamed presence, but they never put a name to that relationship. In short, they've never met Jesus for themselves. They never made the decision to become a disciple of Jesus Christ. They're just name-droppers.

The world has struggled with the growing number of nominal Christians for the past generation. Nominal Christians are those people who are comfortable living within the Judeo-Christian traditions and institutions but live their lives outside the lordship of Jesus Christ. For them, Jesus is just another opinion among many to be considered when making a decision. All of us have a board of directors in our heads that we consult when we have to make important decisions. This board of directors is made up of all the people who have influenced us over our lives and whose opinion of us really matters. Jesus is one of those people, but he is only one. He is important, but he doesn't command our total allegiance. He's a friend, but he is not Lord.

The world has done what the church has been afraid to do. The world won't tolerate nominal Christianity. If we claim to be a believer, the world will demand proof. If your life doesn't show evidence of obedience to the teachings of Christ, the world will simply dismiss the nominal Christian as a fraud and will not take this person seriously. Notice how many well-known television evangelists are mocked by our culture. They aren't mocked because they are too much like Jesus. They're mocked because they aren't like Jesus at all. I'm amazed at how many times the world seems to have a clearer understanding of Jesus, his mission, and his teachings than his own church. Too many of us who claim to know Jesus actually don't. We're quick to drop his name, but we've never actually met him.

In the opening chapters of Acts, Peter and John are told not to preach anymore in the name of Jesus. They answered, "We are unable to stop speaking about what we have seen and heard" (4:20). In the verses leading up to this, we read: "When they [the religious leaders] observed the boldness of Peter and John and realized that they were uneducated and untrained men, they were amazed and recognized that they had been with Jesus" (v. 13). Notice where Peter and John found their authority—not in their education or training, but in their actual experience. In other words, Peter and John may not have known much, but they knew Jesus.

This is where things get interesting for us. Our culture doesn't recognize any objective source of truth. For our society, truth is subjective. This means truth is defined by personal experience. Our neighbors aren't so interested in books about Jesus (even the Bible), but they don't mind listening to someone tell their story, even if that story is about their relationship with Jesus. Many Christians are worried about being tripped up by the conflicts between science and faith or why a good God would allow such evil things to happen in his world. In our discussions with our friends, however, we find out these topics don't come up as much as we think they might. Our friends don't expect us to be expert philosophers. They do, however, expect us to be experts in Jesus. Like Peter and John, we don't have to know a lot about anything else, but we do have to know Jesus.

Before we engage the world, we must understand our own journey, our own story. We have to know our own story before we can tell it to someone else. We have to know *who* we know before we can tell someone else what we know. I know that's a little confusing, but it's true. You have to be sure you *know* something and most of us simply aren't sure. Why not? Because we've never taken the time to process our experience so we fully understand—well, as much as we can understand—the grace of Christ, and as a result, we struggle to communicate what Christ has done for us, who Christ is for us, and what Christ is doing in our lives now. Our witness is confused and, therefore, unconvincing. Remember, after his conversion on the road to Damascus, the apostle Paul disappeared into the Arabian desert for three years. Then, after an initial introduction to Peter, he spent another fourteen years in isolation pouring over the Scriptures to make sure he could grasp this work of grace in his life before he began to preach. Ever wonder how Paul was able to connect the ministry and teachings of Jesus to all those passages in the Old Testament? He studied. He worked to understand how the person of Jesus fit into God's story of Abraham, Isaac, and Jacob, and then, into his own story.

Most of us never do the hard work understanding our own gospel experience because we lack understanding of our own experience. Before we engage the world, we have to engage ourselves. We have to understand the gospel and weave it deeply into the fabric of our own lives. We have to know ourselves in the context of the gospel first. As Christians, we are now in Christ. The gospel isn't something that is just happening to us. The gospel is the new reality in which we live. Only when we understand our life in Christ at this level can we share it. The difference is the difference between painting over rotten boards and replacing them with new wood and then painting. In Christ, all things have been made new, not simply repaired. The difference Jesus makes goes all the way through our lives, touching every aspect of our personhood and individuality. It's a transformative change of the person, not a superficial coating of niceness.

So, let's start there. What's your story? When did Jesus become real to you? Have you thought about your own journey? Have you sought to understand it? Have you dug deep enough into the experience to fully comprehend, as much as you can, what difference your conversion made and has made in your life? Interestingly enough, the culture's refusal to insist on objective truth works in our favor. Most of our friends and neighbors aren't interested in a philosophical or even a theological defense of God. They simply want to know our story. They want to know our truth. Once they hear us sharing about what happened when we came to Christ, the next thing they want to know is does Jesus make any difference in our lives? They aren't asking about eternity; what most of our friends want to know is: Does Jesus make any real difference in our lives here and now?

Yes, it's great news that one day we will live with Jesus forever, but there are days that the best news of all is Jesus can help us right here, right now. Jesus can give us the strength we need to forgive someone who has wounded us when the rest of the world says we should give into our hate and take out our vengeance on the one who hurt us. Jesus can make us better husbands, better wives, and better parents by making us better people. In his grace and mercy, we find freedom from our own baggage that now we, thankfully, don't have to pass along to the next generation. Jesus gives us the strength to break family cycles of despair and hopelessness. That can happen right now. The gospel is good news because it gives us a better way to live right here, right now.

Henry Cloud is a well-known clinical psychologist and leadership expert. His book *Boundaries* is a standard among books suggested for those seeking to improve their mental and emotional well-being. He's also a Christian. In the preface of his new book, *Why I Believe,* Dr. Cloud writes something most of us would agree with: "He [God] is real. . . . I want them [his friends] to have a relationship with Him and know how incredible that is. So why is that a problem? Simple . . . I often do not know how to tell them."[3] There's that gap again. The gap between what we know about Jesus on the one hand and what we can say about him on the other. The gap between how true and obvious the presence of God is to us and how strange this concept is to many of our friends. We've all felt this tension. Cloud wrote an entire book to close this gap between God, himself, and his friends: "The first purpose of this book is to share with you my story of God's reality in my life, and the second is to share how those hard questions were resolved in my own soul and brain."[4]

We would do well to pay attention to Dr. Cloud's outline, especially in this cultural era of personal truth. Dr. Cloud begins with his own testimony—this is what happened to

3. Henry Cloud, *Why I Believe: A Psychologist's Thoughts on Suffering, Miracles, Science, and Faith* (Worthy Publishing, 2024), 1.
4. Cloud, *Why I Believe*, 8.

me. He's not pushing anything on anyone. He's not judging anyone or making anyone feel uncomfortable. He's simply saying you might want to know this about me since you are my friend.

After sharing his decision to become a follower of Christ, Dr. Cloud then begins to work through the difficult questions every believer thinks about. Questions about suffering, the supposed conflict between science and faith, the reality of miracles in his life—he carefully works through each one from his own perspective and experience. Dr. Cloud is a well-educated and thoughtful teacher. What I found interesting was his humility in telling his story and the gentleness in his discussion of the difficult topics that followed. Here is what I've found to be true for me, Dr. Cloud seems to be saying, perhaps my friends will find it true for them. We would all agree there is an objective truth that stands alone outside of our validation, but Dr. Cloud invites his friends to discover this truth for themselves. He encourages his friends to make his truth, *the* truth, their truth.

Rosaria Champagne Butterfield was a lesbian professor of English at a major university when a local pastor began to share the gospel with her. This pastor, Dr. Ken Smith, kept the conversation going for several years. Sometimes he would ask her to read a book, and they would discuss it later. Sometimes he would give her a question to think about. Sometimes she would be invited to join a group having dinner in the pastor's home. Pastor Ken Smith was never overbearing, never desperate for her to make a decision. He was patient, almost like he was confident that, sooner or later, Butterfield would come around to the truth. Eventually, like a sunrise, the light of Christ got brighter and brighter for her. She writes:

> "How did the Lord heal me? The way that he always heals: the word of God got to be bigger inside me than I. My natural inclination was to resist, so like a reflex, I did this. God's people surrounded me. Not to manipulate. Not to badger. But to love and to listen and to watch and to pray. And eventually instead of resisting, I surrendered."[5]

Again, as you read her book, you will see that receiving the gospel took her a long time. Her transformation is still ongoing—as it is for every believer—and it's taking a lifetime. Evangelicals have fallen in love with stories of dramatic and instantaneous conversions such as the apostle Paul's on the road to Damascus. Most conversions, however, are slower and more gradual. First, there's a moment of doubt or confusion. That's followed by questions and discussions with friends who are believers. The frustration grows and the seeker begins to fear they'll never figure it out and then, like a sunrise, the moment that was totally dark is filled with light. Believers must learn not to lose hope when we are walking with our friends. Sometimes conversions are slow and gradual. Like farmers in Jesus's stories, we must carefully tend our plants

---

5. Rosaria Champagne Butterfield, *The Secret Thoughts of an Unlikely Convert: An English Professor's Journey into Christian Faith* (Pittsburgh: Crown & Covenant Publications, 2012).

until they bear fruit. We have to patiently tend to our friends until the gospel bears its fruit in them.

This means we need to be open to whomever the Spirit is engaging at any moment. Sometimes we'll be surprised by those who are being drawn into the faith. Other times, we'll see the obvious signs of the Spirit's presence. Like Pastor Smith in Butterfield's story, everyone needs a friend to walk with, a guide for the journey and a safe place to work through their questions, fears, and confusion. This brings us to one of the ways preaching is changing in our post-truth world. Sermons aren't forty-five-minute lectures logically presented in a three-point structure. Now, people are looking for a conversation, a give-and-take of experiences and ideas. The post-truth preacher isn't looking for a single moment of recognition, but a series of little moments that gradually add up to a lifetime decision that changes everything. A good sermon is one that keeps the conversation going. Preachers must be patient as well as persistent and always trusting the Spirit to keep opening the doors.

The first book I read like this was C. S. Lewis's *Surprised by Joy.* He writes:

> You must picture me alone in that room in Magdalen, night after night, feeling, whenever my mind lifted even for a second from my work, the steady, unrelenting approach of Him whom I so earnestly desired not to meet. That which I greatly feared had at last come upon me. In the Trinity Term of 1929 I gave in, admitted that God was God, and knelt and

> prayed: perhaps that night, the most dejected and reluctant convert in all England. I did not then see what is now the most shining and obvious thing; the Divine humility which will accept a convert on such terms.[6]

Of course, few people in history have written as well or as thoughtfully as C. S. Lewis. I don't know if anyone would describe their conversion with such language. Personally, I've never forgotten the phrase, "Divine humility" since I read it over forty years ago. While we may not have the ability to write like Cloud, Butterfield, or Lewis, all followers of Christ should take the time to map the progress of our conversion. When did you first start thinking about God? What obstacles or hurdles did you have to overcome? What was the final moment that led to your decision? What decision followed after that?

Most of us haven't mined our own stories for the great truths that are hidden so close to our own hearts. We take our faith for granted. We've been like this most of our lives and, now, it's part of our daily routines. We know what we know. We know what we believe. And yet, when the moment opens in a conversation with a friend, we don't know what to say. We should. Not only should we know what to say, we should expect such opportunities to happen. We should be ready to add a little bit of our story to help our friends as they're trying to find out their own story. We need to understand our own

6. C. S. Lewis, *Surprised by Joy: The Shape of My Early Life* (San Francisco: HarperOne, Reissue edition 2017).

relationship—as much as we can—before we can help anyone else understand their relationship with Christ.

My own story is simple. I grew up in a devoutly Christian home. If the church doors were open, we were there—Sunday morning, Sunday night, and Wednesday night. My mom played the piano and sang in the choir. My dad was a deacon and a Sunday school teacher. The old church hymns are the soundtrack to my life. I learned to love Scripture from watching my father study his Bible as he prepared to teach. When I was about seven years old, I felt as if someone was calling my name, but I didn't hear the voice with my ears. I heard it in the center of my chest.

I talked to my mom about what had happened, and before I knew it, she had called the pastor of our little church. He came over one afternoon and walked through the plan of salvation, as we called it, and asked me if I wanted to accept Jesus in my heart. I said yes and was baptized a few weeks later. I was seven years old, and while my decision to follow Christ was as sincere as any seven-year-old's decision could be, I had no idea about the depth of the decision I had just made. I was too young to have any sins to be forgiven. Sure, I told my share of childhood lies and ate cookies Mom told me not to eat, but my conversion was from my sin and to Jesus. I wanted to be like Jesus. That's how my journey with Christ began.

Just as I didn't know the depth of the decision I was making when I decided to follow Christ, I am continuing to learn the depth of the work Christ is doing in me. First, I began to learn what it meant to find my identity in Christ. This didn't mean I simply told people I was a Christian, but I began to understand who I was in terms of how Christ had created me, gifted me, and how he wanted to use my life in the service of his kingdom. I began to understand I was created on purpose for a purpose. In Christ's love, I was complete. I didn't lack anything of meaning in my life. I didn't have to prove anything, accomplish anything, or do anything. I was given a salvation—in the fullest sense of that word—I could never earn, but only accept through faith.

My life was given a purpose of being part of God's redemptive work. My purpose was to find ways to communicate the love of God to each of my neighbors and friends. Of course, I ended up being a pastor, but the essential mission of communicating the love of Christ to a broken world didn't change. Every believer, and I was one of those, has this simple purpose. While I ended up being a pastor, there were many ways I could have expressed my calling to be a communicator of grace. Now that I've stepped away from full-time leadership in the local church, I'm still using my gifts to tell others about Jesus. I'm writing. I blog and I spend a lot of time working with pastors and local churches. The message always remains the same. The method, however, can often change—and does—as new needs and opportunities arise.

Like I said earlier, I wasn't old enough to have committed too many sins (that was to come later), but forgiveness became part of my vocabulary. Not only was I forgiven, but I was also able to forgive. Yes, there were times when I was disobedient and rebellious against the claims of Jesus in my life, but I didn't have what one would call a dramatic testimony.

Through the influence of my family, I was always aware of the presence of Jesus in my life. One of my issues growing up was that I didn't have a dramatic testimony. My life was kind of boring. I kept thinking that if I was going to do anything significant for Christ, I would need to have a more dramatic testimony, but I didn't. My life was a pretty good one.

There was nothing dramatic about my call to the ministry. I simply thought that telling everyone else how much Jesus loved them was the best way to live my life. Those who have heard me tell my story have heard me say that I've never had a crisis of faith. I've always known Jesus was real. My crises have been crises of obedience. There have been times, too many of them, when I simply didn't want to do what Christ was asking me to do. But that's another story.

So, how about your story? Have you thought about it? Let's do that now. Get out a piece of paper. I know, you want to do this on a computer or tablet, but it works better with a pen in hand. Now, write out your story of your conversion. Focus on your conversion. We'll add the rest of the story later, but let's talk about how Christ became real to us. Keep the language simple. Remember, most newspapers are written for the reading level of an average sixteen-year-old American student. Keep it short. This isn't a spiritual biography. This is a short telling of how you came to know Christ. Where were you? What changed for you? How did you know Christ was real to you? Use simple, non-church language as if you were explaining it to a child.

Now, add significant moments from your journey. The gospel is made up of three parts. Justification is the process of being made right with God in Christ. This is the beginning. Glorification is the last part and celebrates God completing his kingdom work in us and all of creation. Sanctification is the middle part of the gospel, and it describes the daily process of being made more like Christ. Right now, at this time in our society, this part of the story is where most of our neighbors will want to begin. They want to hear from us about how Jesus makes a real difference in our everyday lives. Can Jesus help me in my marriage? Can Jesus help me be a better parent? Some of our friends don't have good relationships with their parents. Can Jesus help with that? What if their parents abandoned them? Abused them? Can Jesus help our friends work through their needed healing when life has dealt them hard things?

Has Jesus helped with the real and hard things of everyday life? What are our stories where Jesus has helped us in our day-to-day living? Again, keep it short, but be willing to be as transparent as you're comfortable being telling the story of how Jesus brought you through the tough times in your marriage, in your career—whatever it is. Our friends want to know one thing: "Does it work?" Did it work for us? Will it work for them?

Tell your story. Tell it simply. Our calling is to tell how we have seen Jesus work in our lives. Like Peter and John, we can only testify about what we have seen and heard. We've seen Jesus work. We're sure what we know to be true of Jesus can be true for our friends.

If they'll only make the choice.

Chapter 6

We're Not Stuck

Bronnie Ware would talk to the patients under her care in her hospice practice. They would talk about their lives—their careers and travels, their accomplishments and failures. They would also share their regrets—things they should have done and, of course, things they wish they hadn't done. Ware began to pay attention to the type of things people regretted, and the number-one regret? Not living the life the person wanted to live. For whatever reason, social or family pressure, lack of opportunity, or any number of reasons that in the end didn't seem to matter, the number-one regret was not having the courage to live the life the person wanted to live. The regret wasn't that they didn't live a grand life, but they simply didn't live the life they had envisioned for themselves. They stayed in an unsatisfying relationship. They felt trapped in a dead-end career. Even when they realized they were unhappy, they didn't feel like they had the power to choose a different path. They felt stuck.

One of the first challenges we'll face with our friends and neighbors is that many of them don't feel any power of personal agency. They don't feel like they have a choice, or they feel like they can't make a decision that will actually change anything. So, they don't choose. They just go wherever life takes them, and the currents of culture rarely take us to the places we want to go. Nothing gets better when left unattended. Cars rust and fall apart without maintenance. Houses rot and eventually crumble when they're not kept up. Lives do the same. Lives will eventually fall apart or drift off course without constant attention. This means not only do we have to make one choice, we have to keep making choices. Like a ship sailing in the ocean, we have to keep adjusting our course to counter the currents and tides of the ocean. If we want to live a certain way, we have to first choose to live that way, and then keep choosing that way against the prevailing currents of our culture.

Yes, that's frustrating and fatiguing. No decision is once and for all. We must first choose the life we want, and then we have to keep on choosing to keep our lives moving in the direction of our desired goals. One of the first parts of the good news is that Jesus, through the power of his resurrection, gives us the power to choose the life we want by first "unchoosing" all of the other decisions we've made before choosing to follow him. Like I said, few decisions we make are forever, even wrong decisions we've made in the past that we think now hold us captive. Jesus restores our individual agency. Jesus sets us free from the consequences of not only our own choices, but choices other people have made that have hurt us. We don't have to live as slaves of consequences, either our own or someone else's. Jesus gives us the radical power of choice and the equally radical freedom to make those choices.

Not only that, but the presence of Jesus forces us to make a choice. We'll choose to reject him or we'll choose to follow him, but either way, we'll make a decision. Then, for better or worse, Jesus will allow us to live with the decision we've made. From the earliest pages of the Scriptures, we're taken aback by how seriously Jesus takes our decisions. If we decide to walk with him, he welcomes us along for the journey. If we choose to walk away from Jesus, he allows us to keep walking and won't try to stop us. He grants us the right to make our own choices and then gives us the responsibility to live with the consequences of our choices. From the beginning, God made it clear he didn't want a relationship with robots who had no choice. No, his creation would have a choice, and he wanted his creation to choose to be with him, but he would never force them.

The gospels tell us the story of a financially well-off young man we call "The Rich Young Ruler." A man comes to Jesus and asks Jesus what he has to do to inherit eternal life. Jesus discerns the young man is well meaning and very serious about his faith and his question. Jesus says to the young man that you know the law so keep the commandments. The young man replies he has kept the law since he was a young boy. I've always found it interesting that Jesus doesn't challenge his answer. I fully expected Jesus to say, "No, you haven't!" and then give the man a long list of all his failures. But Jesus lets his reply stand.

Still, he doesn't let the young man off of the hook. "You lack one thing," Jesus told him. "Sell everything you have, give it to the poor, and come follow me." Now, understand the moment. This is the same call that was extended to Peter, John, Matthew, and the rest of the disciples. "Leave your nets." "Leave your tax collection office." "Leave your riches—leave everything and come follow me." This was the same call the other disciples had received. The rich, young ruler was called to be the thirteenth disciple. Everyone else had followed. Everyone but this guy. The story tells us the young man hesitated and then simply walked away. I fully expected the next part of the story to say that Jesus ran after the man and begged him to come back. Jesus doesn't do that. Jesus lets him walk away. The young man made his choice and Jesus wouldn't try to change his mind. The young man would live with the consequences.

In Genesis, Cain is warned by God that sin was crouching at Cain's door, but Cain would have to choose. We know Cain's choices. He made the wrong decision and had to live with the consequences of his choice to murder his brother. Judas made the choice to betray Jesus and his consequences proved to be more than he could live with. Even Zacchaeus, the tax collector who climbed a tree to see Jesus, had to make a choice when Jesus called his name and told him to come down. Every eye in the crowd was now on the tax collector. What would he do? Would he come down or would he stay in the tree? Jesus was just passing by as the Bible tells us. Zacchaeus had to choose to come down from the tree or Jesus would have kept walking and Zacchaeus would have made his decision.

Over and over again, throughout the Bible, God calls on people to choose. As we read, we see the same crossroads again and again. God gives us options, alternatives from which we have to choose. We can go this way or that way. One way leads to this destination and the other leads to another. If we refuse to make a decision, that's a decision too. We'll simply stay where we are. While we may not go to the place God didn't want us to go, we won't get to the place God wants us to go. We'll simply stay where we are, and that's just as bad. To have the choice and not make the choice means you rejected the choice offered by Christ.

In Mark Twain's *Letters from the Earth*, Adam and Eve are keeping diaries about what they discovered about the world in which they live. In one letter, Eve describes her frustration when Adam announces he has discovered water always runs downhill. Adam, Eve later finds out, has been sneaking off to run experiments by himself and, now, he's sure of it. Water always runs downhill. If Adam had kept running experiments, he would have found out everything runs downhill. Nothing gets better on its own. Anything that is neglected decays. That goes for old houses and for human lives. If we don't choose to live well and then keep on not choosing to live well, we'll flow downhill with everything else in our world.

This first part of the good news is this: we have a choice. No matter the situation or the circumstances of our lives, we aren't stuck. We have a choice. We can stay where we are, or we can do something about our circumstances. Jesus gives us this choice. In Christ's coming to our world, he broke the chains of our slavery and invites us to join him on salvation's road to freedom. His light pushed back the darkness. His grace removed the stains of our sins. We don't have to keep making the same mistakes. We can live differently. He gives us the choice to leave our slavery of the world's sinfulness and become fully alive by following him. We are not trapped. We are not victims. We make choices and become the sum total of the choices we've made in obedience to Christ.

According to the way the world sees things, we don't have a choice. Scientism (which claims that *all* things can be known through science) tells us we are nothing more than animal instincts and primitive urges. We are the products of our DNA. Nothing more and nothing less. Evolution has put us in the position to best survive in our world. Our choices are nothing more than dressed up versions of the same decisions we've always made—finding something to eat, finding something to drink, finding a safe place to live and a partner to have children with to ensure the survival of the species. I'm exaggerating a little, but not by much. Many theories of human development have concluded that human beings don't have free will at all and, thus, our ability to make choices is an illusion. If we don't have the capacity to choose, then how can we be responsible for our choices? I think we know, even from our smallest wrong decisions, we end up being held accountable for all of our choices to some degree.

These days, we face a unique challenge with social media. In the last few years, we have developed instruments such as smartphones and tablets that place an almost infinite amount of information at our fingertips, or I should say, in front of our faces. Facebook, TikTok, Instagram, and others are programmed to quickly identify the user's preferences and continue to feed them content to keep them scrolling. These social media platforms make their money when people engage with this media and spend more and more time scrolling down their screens. Social media is successful when we do nothing other than watch other people on the screen. Get that, the less we do, the more successful these platforms are. We end up never making a decision. What the user intends to be a few minutes for a mental break ends up being hours lost to scrolling. Sociologists and psychologists who study mental development of young people now talk in terms of addiction. Parents who have taken their teenagers' phones from them have seen their children melt down in anxiety. These days, we have alarms that go off if we become separated from our phones.

Our world seems determined to overwhelm us with distractions. The good news of our internet-connected world is that we have access to all the knowledge that has ever been available in the world. With a few keystrokes, we can find Lincoln's "Gettysburg Address." We can examine the latest images of space from the Hubble telescope. Much of the information we can find on our pocket computers is interesting and even helpful. If you're like me and not handy around the house, we can find a YouTube video that will show you how to do everything from basic plumbing repairs to connecting the computer and running the most advanced software platforms. While there are hours and hours of helpful and positive content, there seems to be even more hateful, evil, and even silly content. How many cat videos are on these platforms? How many cute babies? How many conspiracy theories or money-making tricks? How many other things are on these platforms that we don't need to know anything about? How much time do we have to waste watching videos that add nothing to the quality of our lives? We're wasting entire lifetimes because our screens keep us so distracted we never choose to do anything else.

The first thing we must do for ourselves and for our friends is to understand that we have the power to choose. With that power to choose comes the responsibility of our consequences. This is a hard point for all of us to understand. Our lives are the sum totals of the decisions we've made throughout our lives. If we find ourselves unhappy in our lives, then we need to take responsibility for those decisions and begin to make different decisions. If we feel like we're stuck in our career, we need to make other decisions. This requires us to do a very tough self-assessment. What do we not like about our job? Do we have the talent to do the job we're in? Is this the place we dreamed about being at this stage in our lives? Do we want to be different?

Then, that requires a choice. This could be everything from looking at job postings to considering going back to school. This choice could also be to choose to stay in your current job because you choose to do so. I know many friends who are in jobs they don't particularly like because the job allows them to balance their lives in ways that work for them. Perhaps their spouse has a job that demands certain things from them. Perhaps the spouse is in school or some kind of career training. I'm thinking about military spouses who move with their spouse from base to base, adapting their careers with every move. Their job doesn't make them happy necessarily, but it works for the family and, thus, it works for them. That's their choice.

Some of us are victims of past abuse. The abuse and neglect were so overwhelming they continue to impact how we're living now. We find ourselves unable to sustain relationships. We're filled with self-loathing and blame. No matter what happens in our lives, we seem to be forever trapped in the role of victim. Jesus gives us a choice. Just as Christ was buried, we, too, have been buried under the evil of someone else's decision. Maybe when we were younger, we didn't have the power to fight back; the power of the resurrected Jesus gives us the power to overcome our wounds and the injuries caused by others. The same power that called Jesus from the grave now calls us. We can choose to follow.

We might think this would be easy enough. I mean, all we have to do is to see where we want to go, who we want to be, and then choose to head in the direction of our goals. It's not that easy. For one thing, we're not isolated beings. We live in a web of relationships with other people; institutions and their combined expectations can make decisions difficult. Sometimes the choice to make a choice can be the most difficult decision of all. Our parents have expectations. In some families, the pressure is to make sure you not only succeed, but succeed to expected levels. Being a doctor isn't enough. Success in some families means you have to be chief of surgery.

No matter how great your success, the family always sees you as a failure.

In other families, success is never recognized at all. The family narrative is about suffering and bad luck. Nothing ever works out for anyone in this family, the children are told, just look at your father or mother (go on down the entire family tree). No one has ever amounted to anything in this family, the family insists, and therefore, you won't amount to anything either. If a child dares to try and break this family narrative, they will find the family openly hostile to their efforts. An alcoholic tries to get sober, and it seems the entire family tries to sabotage their sobriety. Why? Because if someone in the family gets well that puts pressure on everyone in the family to get well. If one person can make a decision and see their life changed, then everybody can. Sometimes, in families, even in local communities, there's pressure not to challenge the prevailing narrative. The person who decided to choose will have to understand the pressure they might encounter from those closest to them.

The world plays a double dirty trick on us. First, the world tells us we can be whatever we want to be. No, we can't. Growing up in Alabama, I wanted to play football for Bear Bryant at the University of Alabama. As far as I know, Coach Bryant never considered that to be a possibility. I was too small. I was too slow. Whatever Coach Bryant was looking for, I was, well, not it! There was nothing I could do about most of that. It was a matter of biology. Unless I chose another mother and father, I would never play football at that level. That's the first trick.

The second trick is to tell me I didn't really want it. If I had truly wanted to play college football, I should have been willing to pay the price. I should have lifted weights. I should have run miles and miles. The American narrative says we can be whatever we want to be if we really want it. Reality says something different. All of us have certain gifts and certain abilities. None of us have *all* of the talents and gifts. Since we are designed for a certain purpose in our lives, we have abilities and talents that match those gifts.

Jesus, on the other hand, tells us something else. He doesn't tell us, "You can be." He says, "You are." In Matthew 16, Jesus asks the disciples who the people think he is. They gave a series of answers. Then, Jesus asks them who they thought he was, and Peter said, "You are the Christ" (v. 16 NASB1995). Jesus celebrates Peter's answer by telling him, "You are the rock." Not, "Peter, you can be a rock," but, "Peter, this is who you are." "We are." Our decisions are made not from who we hope we can be, but who God has already called us to be. Because Peter was the rock, he could find the strength he needed to overcome his failure after the arrest of Jesus and become a leader of the new church.

What was good news to Peter will now become good news to us. Whatever we lack, the Spirit will provide. As pastors and preachers, we'll find ourselves able to stay in the conversation a little longer than we thought. We'll be able to love friends and neighbors because Christ has loved us first. We are the messengers Jesus sent us to be. In Christ, we have already become what we wanted to become.

This gift is offered to our friends as well. In this moment, their choices and decisions can lead them to the life they want. But first, we have to decide what we want. We'll talk about that next.

Chapter 7

What Do You Want?

Once when I was playing golf with a friend named Alex, I learned one of life's most important lessons. Alex was a serious golfer. He would talk about the physics of a golf ball flying through the air and the different flight patterns of differently shaped dimples in the ball.

On this particular day, Alex and I were teeing off, and as usual, he crushed his ball straight down the fairway. Then I hit my ball and it went . . . well, let's just say, it went. Alex laughed at me. If you're not familiar with golf etiquette, it's considered impolite to laugh at another player's poor shot. You're expected to say something like, "Tough luck," or, "I think we can find your ball over there," but never are you permitted to laugh.

Alex laughed. When I asked him what he was laughing at, he said he was laughing at me. "Why are you laughing at me?"

"Because," he said, "you don't do anything in your swing to make the ball go where you want it to go. You just stand up here and wish."

And that was the moment I learned there is a difference between wishing and wanting. What's the difference? Wishing means you'd like for good things to happen, but you aren't going to take any action to make your desired wish come true. Wanting means you'd like for something to happen and you're willing to take the necessary actions to make those desires become a reality. For instance, if you want to play better golf, you take the necessary steps. You hire a coach. You hit practice balls at the range. Those are the things you do if you *want* to get better. If you aren't doing those things, you're just wishing.

Most of us are wishing. For one thing, we've never sat down long enough to seriously think about what we want. We just make a decision in the moment and hope it works out for the best. If it doesn't, then we'll make another decision. So it goes for the rest of our lives. We never choose to really *go* anywhere; we meander through life. Most of us end up disappointed that we didn't get to the place or places we actually wanted to go. We end up wishing away our lives. Too many times our lives resemble a typical couple going out to dinner. No one made reservations. No one thought that far ahead. The husband asks his wife where she wants to go to dinner, and she says that she doesn't care. They can go anywhere to eat. Everyone knows what happens next. The couple ends up fighting because they can't agree on what they want to eat, much less which restaurant to eat at. They'll end up going back home and making sandwiches. All this happens because no one knows what they want.

So, here's an obvious question: What do we want out of our lives? What kind of lives do we want to live? How would we answer if God himself were to ask us what we wanted? Sounds like a bad movie with a genie and a magic lamp. We rub the lamp and suddenly a genie appears in a puff of smoke and gives us three wishes. Believe it or not, there are times when God does ask his people what we would want from him.

One of the most familiar is the story of Solomon. Solomon has just become king following his father, David. At Gibeon, God appeared to Solomon and asked the young king what he wanted as he began his reign. Famously, Solomon asked for wisdom so he could be a good king for his people. Moved by his response, God not only gave Solomon the wisdom he requested, but riches and power as well. How would the story be different if God had asked one of us? How would God have responded if we had answered, "Can we get back to you?"

A lot of our congregations simply don't know what they want. They've never thought about it. They're too busy with the daily grind. If they ever do think about it, they find themselves told by the world around them that what they want is stupid or too impossible to even dream about. Too many of our friends end up wanting what they don't want because they're trying to please everyone else. Or they lack the courage to try to attain what they want and it ends up just a wish.

The Gospel of John tells us about a conversation between Jesus and his first disciples. When the disciples found Jesus, he asked them a question: "What do you want?" This is a dangerous question. I know it doesn't sound that ominous, but think about it. What if the disciples gave Jesus the wrong answer? What if Jesus gave us what we asked of him, only to later realize that what we thought we wanted isn't what we wanted all? How many times has this happened? We finally buy the one thing we think will make us happy, and the happiness lasts about as long as our attention span. Soon, our favorite possession is in a box on the way to the recycling center.

Have we ever done the intentional work of putting down on paper what we want our lives to look like? Who do we want to become? What kind of marriage do we want? Do we even want to get married? Not everyone wants to get married nor should everyone get married. What career should we pursue? Where do we want to live? Would you prefer to live in the city or the suburbs? In his book *The Paradox of Choice*, Barry Schwartz suggests we have so many choices in our lives that require so many decisions day after day, that we actually become too tired to make any more decisions.[7] We become so overwhelmed by our options we can't make any decisions. We have so many choices that we don't have any choices at all. This is the kind of tension that fills the minds of those that fill the seats in our sanctuaries.

We don't need to worry about that too much. After all, a lot of our decisions make themselves. In reality, we aren't choosing from every available option in the universe, we are choosing from choices from a select group. For instance, when

---

7. Barry Schwartz, *The Paradox of Choice: Why More Is Less* (New York: HarperCollins, 2016), 21.

I go and shop for clothes, I'm not looking at everything everybody wears all over the world. I live in the American south. It's hot where I live. I typically avoid sweaters or anything fur-lined. I'm wearing pants, most likely cotton or wool. I will wear khaki-, black-, blue-, or gray-colored slacks, and only certain shades of those colors. So, in a matter of seconds, I've limited my choices in clothes, and yet, I don't feel deprived in any way.

It's the same way with most of our decisions. While the options may seem endless, in reality, they are not. There are a lot of careers, but I either can't or don't want to do a lot of them. I love watching *Deadliest Catch* on television, but I have no desire to work on a crab boat in the Bering Sea. I'd love to play in a rock-and-roll band, but that's not an option either. So, for all my choices of careers, I really only have a few to choose from. I went to college thinking I would go to law school. I ended up going to seminary. My career choices fell within a very narrow range of options. It's the same with everyone and every decision. The popular myth is you can have anything you want, do anything you want, or be anything you want—but you can't. No one can.

In the great scheme of things, only a handful of decisions end up making any real difference in our lives, and those are hard enough. For instance, when asked, most people will say, "I just want to be happy." That sounds nice until we drill down and try to understand what happiness means. When we ask people what they mean when they say "happy," most don't have a real understanding. They don't have a goal, a target. It's like they're on this long journey called life without any particular destination. Despite all our anxiety over decisions and choices, most of us end up never really deciding. We don't know what we want, so it doesn't matter what we do. We don't end up going where we wanted to go and our drifting through life never brings us to our purpose and meaning. We end up disappointed and angry at having missed our one chance to make our lives count.

The challenge of preaching is to help our friends and neighbors sift through the distractions of our world and begin to focus on those things that really matter. In her book *10-10-10,* Susan Welch tells us to begin to ask ourselves what does our future self want us to do at this moment? Can we take ten minutes to think about what we will be dealing with in ten months? Ten years?[8] Can we think through how the decisions we're making right now will affect us in our future lives? A lot of people don't understand that the decisions they are making today determine who they will become tomorrow. As pastors, we're privileged to sit with our people while they sift through the mud of the world's sludge, like a forty-niner gold miner, to find the nuggets of gold remaining in our pans. We're there when they discover what really matters in their lives, when they hold those things that will last.

A few years ago, I was talking to a young man about where he wanted to go in his life. When I asked him about his five-year plan, he said he wanted to be married and working in his career. So far, so good. Then I asked him about the young women he was dating at the time. "Are any of these

8. Susan Welch, *10-10-10: A Life-Transforming Idea* (New York: Scribner, 2010), 9.

young women you're currently dating the kind of woman you'd like to marry one day?" He looked at me, and I could see the disappointment register on his face. Disappointment is an understatement. The better word would be *shock*. "No," he said. "Well," I asked, "why aren't you dating the kind of women you'd one day like to marry?" The truth was painful, but honest. "None of the girls that I think would make good wives will go out with me."

Hard moment, but his honesty gave us a good place to start. First, he needed to stop dating the young women he was dating and start working on being the kind of man women would want to one day marry. "Stop looking for Miss Right," I told him, "and start working on becoming Mister Right." Become a young man of character and integrity. Put a life plan together and show the young women you're dating you have purpose in your life. Be a man who's going somewhere. Just those qualities alone will make you a more attractive man. He ended up doing well. He's married, a father of two children, and very successful in his insurance business in Indiana. None of that started, however, until he made the decision about where he was going and the steps required to get him where he wanted to go.

One of the glaring omissions of the church today is that we rarely preach on the middle part of salvation. As many of us know, the word *salvation* in Greek conveys three meanings at the same time. The first part of salvation is being made right with God in Christ. This is when we are forgiven for our sins and given a new life in him. We call that justification. Justification is a building term that means "to align." When a builder puts up a vertical beam, they will check to make sure the beam is straight. Builders used to use a plumb line to do this. A plumb line was held in the air and the beam was moved left or right so it aligned with the plumb line. (Now we do this with lasers, but I'm old enough to remember using a plumb line.) That process of alignment is called justification.

The third part of salvation is called glorification, and it celebrates the completion of God's redemptive work not only in his people, but in all of creation. According to Paul, every part of creation longs for this moment. For most critics of Christianity, this promise of a "better life by and by" dismisses the suffering and injustices currently being endured by too many people. Preaching that God will take care of everything that is wrong in our world one day, someday, often allows the church to ignore the pain of our neighbors. That would be true if glorification was all that we hoped for as Christ followers.

But there's more—a lot more. There's the whole wondrous middle part of the Christian journey called sanctification. From the point we encounter Christ to the point where Christ makes everything new, we are being made more and more into the likeness of Christ. We are being sanctified. We are being made holy. That is, everything in our lives that doesn't look like Christ is removed from our lives and things that we lack are added to our lives. Every part of our lives is impacted by this process. The way we think, the things we desire, our communities, and our priorities are all transformed. This is a daily, lifelong journey. Having our hearts changed to love as Christ loves, to forgive as he forgives, is no easy feat. Too many of us think making disciples can be made in microwave ovens. We push a few buttons, wait a few seconds, and *Ding!* . . . out comes a disciple.

First, our old ways of living and thinking have to be dismantled and removed from our lives and thought processes. We can't respond in anger the way we used to. We can't be trapped in old tapes that formed our way of thinking about our identity and our values. We can't hide in our addictions from the pain deep within our lives. Jesus wants to set us free from that pain and heal those wounds. That means the slow process of going deep in ourselves and allowing Christ to identify and heal those deep wounds that continue to affect our lives long after they occurred. Maybe we lost a parent when we were young, our parents divorced, or we experienced some kind of financial or health crisis. These events and so many more like them scar us for life. No matter what we do, we always seem to make our decisions in reaction to that one painful moment. Christ heals that moment and rebuilds us from the ground up. We become new people.

How does that happen? For one thing, God isn't limited by a space-time continuum. His timing and presence is unlimited. He's never too late or too early. For God, it's always now, always was, and always will be. "Great," you say, "but what does that have to do with anything?" First, it means God is with us in our present. Second, it means God is waiting for us in our future. The reason we are so confident that our future is as God says it will be is because he's already there waiting on us to join him. Last, it means God is still in our past; he is still there in our past. This means he can go to that moment when we thought our life was destroyed—the stupid decision we made or the cruel thing someone else did to us—and he can heal that moment so that our past wounds no longer bleed into our present.

I can't tell you how many times someone has walked into my office and confessed some past mistake. This admission is humiliating to them and still very difficult for them to talk about without breaking down. Over and over again, they will beg me not to tell anyone. Of course, I tell them I won't tell anyone; that is sacred to the pastoral vocation. We will begin to meet and work through the healing process and Jesus will do what Jesus does. This person will be made whole. They will become a new person visibly changed by the freedom and joy they now have in Christ. Then, they will ask me to come to their small group on a particular night because they are going to share their testimony. I will go and, much to my surprise (though it's happened enough I shouldn't be surprised anymore), they will begin their testimony with the very event they asked me to never tell anyone.

Jesus is so good. He is so strong he can make the worst moment of our lives the first sentence of our testimony.

This is why sanctification is so important for us to understand. This is the process where Jesus begins to change our desires. Because most of us haven't done the hard work of making the decision about what we want out of our lives and because most of us simply drift with the currents of our times, we never end up living the life we wanted or becoming the person we wanted to be. How does Jesus prevent us from hitting a dead end in our lives?

First, he changes what we love. Then, he changes the way we think. And last, he changes us by what we do. This ends up changing who we become. How does God change what we love? Perhaps I should be more specific. He changes us by changing Whom we love. In John 12, we read the story of Mary and her expensive anointing of Jesus:

> Six days before the Passover, Jesus came to Bethany where Lazarus was, the one Jesus had raised from the dead. So they gave a dinner for him there; Martha was serving them, and Lazarus was one of those reclining at the table with him. Then Mary took a pound of perfume, pure and expensive nard, anointed Jesus's feet, and wiped his feet with her hair. So the house was filled with the fragrance of the perfume. (vv. 1–3)

There are all kinds of stories about why Mary would react like this, but let's stick with what we know. Jesus had raised her brother from the dead. The next opportunity she has, she repays him the only way she knows how. She brings the most expensive thing she has and offers it to Jesus. She responds in a moment of extravagant worship. She owed everything to Jesus and her life now revolved around him. The apostle Paul describes his life being poured out, emptied out in service to Christ. His ministry was in response to the crucifixion of Christ for his sins. This is the way all of us respond to Christ. We're overwhelmed by the love and grace of Christ and we offer our own lives in service to him and his kingdom.

Everything we do is first viewed through the lens of our love for Christ.

In Romans 12, Paul writes: "Do not be conformed to this age, but be transformed by the renewing of your mind, so that you may discern what is the good, pleasing, and perfect will of God" (v. 2). In Philippians 4:8, Paul gives instructions to young disciples like us: "Finally brothers and sisters, whatever is true, whatever is honorable, whatever is just, whatever is pure, whatever is lovely, whatever is commendable—if there is any moral excellence and if there is anything praiseworthy—dwell on these things."

We control what we think by controlling our thoughts. I know we've heard that no one can control their thoughts. We just think what we think. The truth is we *can* control what we think. It takes a little work. It takes a little practice, but we can do it. How? By making conscious decisions about what we think about from moment to moment. There have been many studies done on how human beings deal with their attention. Social media makes all their money from controlling what we think about as we scroll through their platforms. In Christ, we have the power to control what we think about, and we do that by choosing to think about things that are beautiful and lovely. In short, we think about things that are of Christ.

Last, Jesus says if we love him then we'll keep his commandments. It's that simple and it's that hard. Our love for Christ isn't about how loud we profess it, but how faithfully we live it. Paul writes in Romans 5: "And not only that, but we also boast in our afflictions, because we know that affliction produces endurance, endurance produces proven character, and proven character produces hope. This hope will not disappoint us, because God's love has been poured out in our hearts through the Holy Spirit who was given to us" (vv. 3–5).

Our decisions, every choice big and small, ends up determining who we are. We choose, day by day, the people we become. Growing up takes time. As much as our culture tries to make us grow up faster than we should, we're becoming more and more convinced that becoming a mature human being just takes time, and you can't rush that. Just look at the debate on when a child should be given a smartphone!

Growing into maturity as a follower of Christ takes a long time. I write this to encourage those of us who are teachers so we don't lose patience with our younger brothers and sisters who are struggling in their newfound faith. I'm also writing to encourage those of us who are new in our relationship with Christ. Don't give up. It just takes time.

Which means, as missionaries to our culture, we have to begin to think more like farmers.

Chapter 8

How Long?

When I was in high school, I had my wisdom teeth removed. Everything went fine with the surgery, and I was home that afternoon. Three days later, however, I woke up and my jaw was so swollen that it looked like I was trying to swallow a baseball. My mom took me back to the oral surgeon, and when he saw me, he laughed and said, "You healed too fast." Healed too fast? I didn't think you could do that. Yet, according to my doctor, you can. As he explained to me, the skin of my gum line had healed and closed the empty socket where my wisdom tooth used to be. The healing of the gum line had trapped all the bacteria in the dark, moist socket—an ideal breeding ground for bacteria—and caused the infection. He reopened the socket and left some gauze in the opening to slow the healing.

As I've dealt with people over the years, I've had several conversations with people who were hurting for all kinds of reasons. Some had made life-altering mistakes. Some were hurt by people they trusted. Sometimes their pain was so intense they couldn't function. Other times, the pain made them numb and unable to feel anything in their lives. As we would talk, it became clear the only thing they wanted was for the pain to go away. They didn't necessarily want to be healed. Not feeling pain and being well are two different things. "Most people just want to get rid of the pain," a counselor friend told me. "They don't want to get well."

Have you ever wondered why Jesus asked the man at the pool of Bethesda if he wanted to get well? When we read the story in John 5, our first reaction is to discount the question. Jesus is trying to get the conversation going. Surely, he's not wondering if the man really wants to get well. Of course, the man wants to get well. Why would Jesus even have to ask? The more we read the story, however, the more we see the validity of Jesus's question. When Jesus asked the man the question, we expected the man to respond with an enthusiastic, "Yes!" but that's not how he answered. Instead, he gives Jesus a long list of reasons of why he can't get into the pool and, thus, why he can't get healed. I've often read this story and thought that if my limitations kept me from getting healed, I'd come up with a plan to get into that pool somehow or someway. Yet, after all this time, he had no plan, only excuses.

Getting well takes a lot of work—emotional, spiritual, and mental. We have to go back to the moment when we failed, disappointed ourselves and others, or were wounded by someone (either intentionally or unintentionally) to fully understand what happened. If we have responsibility in the moment, we have to own our part of the event. If someone else caused the pain, we have to name the pain and eventually forgive them. I say *eventually* because forgiveness is a process. We forgive as much as we can in the moment, but we may have to do this several times over several months or even years. Forgiveness means we have to release the person from the expectation that they can fix what they've done. They can't. Only Jesus can bring that kind of healing. We have to release the other person and bring our pain to Christ in prayer. That's where the healing takes place.

A few years ago, a friend asked me to pray with him about a particular situation in his life. I told him I had become very careful about praying that prayer. When my friend asked why, I told him I had learned that when I pray for Jesus to help me with a problem, he'll throw me directly into the problem. For instance, if I have a problem with someone and I pray for God to help me work things out, I'll find myself running into that person everywhere I go. If I'm getting gas, he'll be at the next pump. If I go to get groceries, he'll be checking out right in front of me. I'll be forced to deal with whatever the issue is—and soon. It took me a long time to figure this out, and finally, I got it. The reason Jesus takes us right through the problem is that once we're through it, we don't have to be afraid of it anymore. This is the only way true healing happens. These things have to be dealt with. They can't be avoided.

In the South, we have problems with dandelions. These weeds, whose seeds fly all over our yards with the slightest breeze, are notoriously hard to kill. When we try to get them out of our yards, we have to be sure we dig up the entire root.

If you don't dig out the root, the dandelion will grow back. Sin, anger, and guilt have deep roots. Jesus wants us to deal with our pain at its roots so that it never returns. We want dealing with our pain to be like walking up a set of stairs. We want to deal with it, step up, and move on. Our pain is more like a spiral. We keep coming back to the same issue, but at a deeper level.

There's a reason Jesus talked so much about agriculture. Growing crops and growing humans have much in common. They both take a lot of work. First, you have to prepare the soil. Then, you have to plant the seed. That's followed by weeks and months of watering, weeding, and fertilizing. Finally, after months of work, we'll be able to harvest the fruit. Humans are the same way. First, our hearts and minds have to be prepared. We have to be in the right frame of mind and heart to be able to receive the gospel. The gospel is then planted with the person's life and, from there, the Spirit begins to nurture the new plants. Only later do we begin to see the birth of a new disciple. Remember Paul's true conversion, the full development of the theology and call, took years. The conversion of Rosaria Champagne Butterfield took years. So did C. S. Lewis's.

While Paul's conversion was dramatic, it was not an instant process. He still went through the process of having Christ meeting him on the road to Damascus, wrestling with temporary blindness, and his eventual meeting with Ananias. While there are many conversions like that, most conversions are much slower and gradual. A friend will think about Christ and his claims for weeks, if not months, before making a decision. We shouldn't be surprised by this. In fact, we should expect it. Growing people takes a long time. Growing disciples takes longer.

Let's look at the story of the prodigal son in Luke 15 to further understand the process. Most of us remember the story. A young son demands his inheritance from his father, and when the father reluctantly gives him the money, the young son leaves home. We're told the young man heads to a far country where he wastes his money in frivolous living. When he is broke, his friends abandon him and he ends up working for a local farmer keeping pigs. While in the pigsty, the young man thinks to himself that his father treats his slaves better than he is living. He decides to go home and ask his father to receive him back, not as a son, but as a slave. When the son is still far away from his house, the father recognizes him and runs out to meet his son. Welcoming his son home, the father throws an extravagant party, dresses his son in the finest robes, and places the family ring on his finger. Not only was the son forgiven, he was restored by his father.

For all of our talk about forgiveness, forgiveness isn't the point. The goal is restoration, a full uniting to our heavenly Father through Jesus Christ. Forgiveness is one step in that process. The goal of the father wasn't to just have his son home, but to have his son home fully restored as a son. Forgiveness is the beginning of the journey, not the end.

When someone comes to Christ, they begin a new journey of becoming an entirely new person. Forgiveness begins the process. The next steps include discovering our true identity in Christ, our giftedness in Christ, and from that, our purpose. We also begin building our character into the likeness of Christ. All of this—justification, sanctification, and glorification—are all part of the salvation process. We have been saved, we will be saved, and we are being saved. The work of the Spirit with each disciple goes on constantly. We are being formed more and more into the likeness of Christ every day. This molding of our character happens gradually, almost imperceptibly. Only after the passage of time can a disciple see how far they have come.

In our post-truth world, we need to see evangelism as a journey, not just one moment. When I was beginning my ministry, we were trained to "lead someone to the Lord." We were given a tract or trained in how to ask a series of questions. As we walked the person through the tract or led them through the questions, the assumption would be that at the end of the conversation, the person would accept Christ. Once that person made a decision to become a follower of Christ, we made sure they were baptized and then moved on to the next person. We were God's hit squad, rounding up people for Jesus and getting them baptized. In Baptist life, that was called "dunk 'em and drop 'em." We would get them started in the journey of discipleship, but we would abandon them at the beginning of their journey. This is spiritual child abuse. If we are truly "born again," that means we are starting all over again. We have to learn everything again, except this time from a kingdom perspective. We have to learn to think again, walk again, speak again—and all of it as a child of God and his kingdom.

Think about a person who's been injured and is being treated for multiple injuries. This person will have a full medical staff and a number of therapists helping them. There will be tests and exercises given to the patient to make sure they push themselves to their limits to guarantee their best life. And who is working with the new believer? Too many times, no one is working with the young disciple. The result is we brag about the number of conversions in our churches, but we don't see a corresponding growth in membership or attendance. Most of our conversions never develop into mature disciples.

Leading someone to Christ is just the first step. We need to understand our evangelistic responsibility doesn't stop when the person comes to Christ. That's just the first step. Now, just as parents of a newborn child are expected to help their child grow into a healthy adult, we in the church need to recognize our responsibility to grow new believers into mature disciples of Christ. That means, as older brothers and sisters, we'll train our little brothers and sisters in the spiritual disciplines such as prayer and Bible study, worship and congregational life. We'll help them understand their spiritual gifts and then walk with them as they understand their giftedness and how they are to use their spiritual gifts in the service of the kingdom. We're to be there when something goes wrong in their lives.

And it will. Most of us who have followed Jesus for a while understand we're most vulnerable in the early days of our discipleship. If the young follower gets knocked off the track early, they may never recover. So, when something goes wrong for them—job loss, family strife, a health crisis—the church must come around this new believer as family and walk them through their troubles.

I'm not sure many in our congregation understand this side of evangelism. One of the metaphors for the early church was family. There are several times when the church is called "the family of God" in the New Testament. New believers are now members of our family. This means we have family obligations toward them, and they have family responsibilities toward us. In a world where too many people grow up in broken homes and the broken promises that caused those homes to break, the church has the privilege to re-parent these young Christians for them to be able to grow up into the fullness of their created potential.

Think about what families do—the best ones, anyway. Our families teach us to control our impulses. Just because we want something doesn't mean we get it. We have to learn patience, self-control, how to handle our anger and disappointment. We must learn the importance of doing chores when the family is counting on us. If we grew up on a farm, we understand the family livelihood counts on each child doing their part whether that was feeding the chickens or watering the horses. Suburban and urban children have their necessary chores as well. It could be doing some of the cooking or cleaning, watching over younger siblings, or doing the laundry. There's no special talent required for any of these chores. They just need to be done so the family can function smoothly.

In the same way, the church family has chores that need to be done. We spend a lot of time thinking about spiritual gifts and how each of us needs to be sure we're using our gifts in the best ways to serve the kingdom. There is no spiritual gift for taking out the garbage. Taking out the garbage may not get you any parades, but without it, sooner or later the church can't function. There are plenty of things that need to be done in the church that don't require anything more than someone willing to do them. When a new believer starts doing even the most basic of tasks in the church, they'll learn the basics of service and family. They'll feel the joy of being needed. After all, if they don't show up to set up the tables for the fellowship dinner, who will?

Brentwood Baptist Church built a gymnasium before we built our first sanctuary. For the worship service to be held in the gym on Sunday morning the chairs had to be set up. Then, for the students and children to skate and play basketball, the chairs had to be stacked up and stored for next Sunday. If you talk to anyone who was part of the church then, they'll talk about being in the "fellowship of the chairs." A friend of mine told me he knew he was a man when his father told him to grab a chair after the worship service was over. The Sunday before, he had been dismissed to go play with the other children. Now, he was a man because he had been told to grab a chair. Others have told me they decided to join Brentwood Baptist Church on the Sunday they ended up helping put the chairs up. Why? They felt the church needed them.

Church growth experts will often say a new member has to be engaged in a meaningful relationship and ministry for them to still be part of the church in five years. Most churches don't have a robust new-member process, and as a result, new members are on their own to find their place in the church. It's hit or miss, and a miss is more likely than not. More important, most Christians don't have an understanding of their responsibility—and, indeed, calling—to work with a new believer until they understand their place to engage for the kingdom of God. Only when the young believer is fully engaged in their own mission, sharing the gospel of Christ with their friends, is the evangelist free from their calling to the new believer. Parents are only relieved of their responsibility when their child is able to take on the responsibilities of an adult.

This takes longer than we think. Most brains aren't fully developed until we're twenty-five years old. As lifespans have lengthened, so each episode within the lifespan has lengthened. My father was a man when he was fourteen. He took the wagon into town to sell crops. He bought supplies for the farm. I was a man when I was eighteen. Now, adolescence ends at thirty. Our society will forgive anything before thirty, but after thirty our society expects us to have our lives figured out. Working with a new believer to grow into a mature disciple takes a long time. Jesus worked with the Twelve for three years. Moses wasn't ready to take on Pharaoh until he was eighty. In the first forty years of Moses's life, he learned how to rule as a child in Pharaoh's court. Forty years after that he learned to live in the desert as Jethro's son-in-law. Only then was Moses ready to lead the Israelites out of Egypt.

When I was in elementary school, my class planted butter beans in milk cartons filled with dirt. We brought our milk cartons back from lunch one day, cut off the top half of the cartons, and filled the cartons with potting soil. We pushed the little beans into the soil and watched them disappear in the dirt. Then, we waited. And after that, we waited some more. Our teachers told us to keep the plants watered, but as far as we could tell, we were just pouring water on dirt. Finally, a little green leaf broke through the soil. We were just about to give up. Over the next few days, we watched the butter bean plant sprout until it was several inches tall. It just took time.

Maybe that's why Jesus talked so much about agriculture. Growing things takes time. Preparing the soil. Planting the seeds. Weeding, watering, and fertilizing—all take a lot of time. Finally, months after planting, the harvest finally comes. Pastors, like farmers, have to be long-suffering and patient. We have to understand there are things in this process we can't control. Sometimes, as much as we pray, the rain doesn't come. Sometimes, as hard as we work, the harvest doesn't come in. What do we do when this happens? Same thing a good farmer does: we plant more seeds and work the field all over again.

Growing people takes a long time. There's the preparation of the heart through prayer and friendship. The planting of the seeds in gentle conversations and discussions. There is the reading of books and studying the Bible to nourish the seeds that have been planted. Finally, if the person allows the Spirit to do his work, a new child of the kingdom is born. I'm writing this chapter to remind those of you on this journey that becoming all Christ is calling you to be takes a long time. There's a lot to learn. Be patient. Growing people in Christ, like growing anything, takes a long time. Don't give up.

Chapter 9

The Laboratory of Life

In the movie *Oppenheimer*, General Leslie Groves, played by Matt Damon, is talking to Oppenheimer about what would happen when the atomic bomb was actually tested. Oppenheimer says there's no way to really know because nothing like this has ever been tried before. Groves mentions that some of the other scientists were talking about some of the possibilities that included the destruction of the world. Oppenheimer agrees. There was a very slight chance that when the bomb was ignited, it would set the atmosphere itself on fire. "Do you mean we could destroy the whole world?" Groves asked. The world didn't blow up and the atomic age was initiated with the use of the atomic bomb in World War II. Groves makes the point that all of us want to know when we're faced with something new. We only have one question: Will it work? Americans, for all of our debates and discussions, are a very practical people. We just want things to work. How many times have you been in a problem-solving group when one of the team will suggest a solution? The solution will be elegant and appear to answer every question that is being posed, and then someone will say, "There's only one problem with that. It won't work."

Believe it or not, that's the question most Americans have about Christianity. They hear the beautiful teachings of Christ and their first response is, "That won't work." If someone hits you on one cheek, turn the other cheek. If someone makes you walk one mile, walk two instead. Really? Does Jesus really say that? Most people hear those statements and many others from Jesus, and just shake their heads. In this dog-eat-dog world, people think being kind and gracious makes them look weak. They fear they'll be taken advantage of, used, and well, overrun by the bullies of our world. Many evangelicals live by one creed on Sunday and another creed on Monday. Why? Because we don't think the teachings of Jesus will work in the real world. They sound great, but they don't work.

My initial reply to this criticism is this. When Jesus cleaned out the temple, no one challenged his actions. Now, think about that. He walked into people's places of business—tents filled with animals, tables filled with coins—and threw everything up in the air. Can you imagine the chaos? Coins flying in the air and hitting the ground. Birds flying off and sheep running for shelter. In the middle of this storm stood Jesus, and no one confronted him. The temple guards didn't move. The business owners didn't try to stop him. Why? First of all, Jesus was probably a more imposing figure than we usually imagine him to be. He was a carpenter. Some scholars translate the word *carpenter* to *builder*, which means Jesus would have worked with stone. Either way, Jesus would have worked with his hands. He would have been stronger than most of us assume. Second, there would have been something in the fierceness of Jesus that would have discouraged people from coming at him.

I'm not trying to play the "my Daddy can beat up your daddy" game. I am, however, challenging the common myth that following Jesus makes one too weak to engage and overcome life's challenges. The very life of Jesus disproves this point. During his torture and crucifixion, Jesus endured an enormous beating, finally collapsing while carrying his cross to the place of his execution. Whatever we have been thinking of Jesus and the way he lived life, we probably need to adjust our thinking about him. Jesus is more than we can imagine in every aspect of his life and in every aspect of how he lived.

While we're on the attributes of Jesus, Dallas Willard wrote, when speaking of Jesus, that one of our foundational assumptions about him has to be that Jesus was the smartest man to ever live. "Can we seriously imagine that Jesus could be *LORD* if he were not smart? If he were divine, would he be dumb? Or uninformed? Once you stop and think about it, how could he be what we take him to be in all other respects and not be the best-informed and most intelligent person of all, the smartest person to ever live?"[9] That is, Jesus knows more about life and what makes it worth living than anyone else who has ever lived. Yes, Jesus understands physics and geology. Yes, Jesus understands history and economics. More

9. Dallas Willard, *The Divine Conspiracy: Rediscovering Our Hidden Life in Christ* (New York: Harper Collins, 1998), 94.

than that, however, Jesus understands purpose and meaning at deeper levels than any other human who has ever lived and who will ever live in the future.

Christianity makes some alarming claims about itself. Not only does it promise living forever with God himself, but it also claims to be the best way to live in our present world. In Matthew 11:28–30, Jesus says, "Come to Me, all who are weary and heavy-laden, and I will give you rest. Take My yoke upon you and learn from Me, for I am gentle and humble in heart, and you will find rest for your souls. For My yoke is easy and My burden is light" (NASB1995). The language is more intimate than the English translation suggests. Jesus isn't talking about having an easy life. He's talking about a life that fits. The yoke Jesus mentions is for work, to be sure, but it's a well-fitted yoke. This yoke has been altered to fit us and us alone. Whatever our task, it is well-tailored for us. The rest Jesus talks about isn't about sleeping late, but being aligned with our kingdom calling so our lives are joyful and peaceful, free from anxiety. We can rest at night knowing our work and our lives are making a difference.

To our previous point, how does this work?

The gospel begins with our humanity. The Bible is always very clear. We are created beings. We are human. We were never gods. We were never created to be gods. We were made from the earth and filled with the breath of God, but we were always limited. We were limited by time and space. We were limited by knowledge and abilities. This immediately conflicts with the world's myth that we can do anything we want if we just believe enough, work hard enough, etc. Don't get me wrong. Human beings have enormous potential. I believe God enjoys our discoveries and inventions. Like our Father, human beings are creative and imaginative. Yet, unlike God, we have limits. We can't work for very long without food, water, or rest. We can't thrive very well without communities. This is a very important teaching for us to fully understand. We're not God. We were never intended to be. We can relax knowing all of creation doesn't depend on us. We can simply be who the Creator made us to be.

This good news goes for us as well. As pastors and preachers, we need to remember that everything doesn't depend on us. We are free to simply share the good news of Jesus the best way we know how and trust the Spirit with the rest. We can experience the joy of Jesus's presence every day and rest in that peace. We simply tell what happened when we met Jesus and how our lives have been changed and are being changed by him. We simply tell what we know to be true in our own lives. The telling, like the news itself, is supposed to be joyful.

While we were never intended to be God, we were created to be with God. The main purpose of our lives is to be with God and enjoy his presence. Period. That's it. This grand purpose of being with God aligns all the other choices we must make day in and day out. This happens because our purpose of being with Jesus leads us to a single question that funnels us to every decision we make. That question is: "Does this bring me closer to Jesus or does it take me further away from Jesus?" This divine focus on our lives renders most questions irrelevant. I don't think Jesus cares what kind of pants I wear. Whether I choose jeans, khakis, or expensive wool blends, it doesn't matter. Most of our questions in our lives don't matter because they aren't eternally significant. They simply don't matter. This gives us a lot of freedom and takes off a lot of pressure.

Obviously, if something isn't helpful to drawing us near to Christ, don't do it. As the apostle Paul writes: "'All things are lawful,' but not all things are helpful" (1 Cor. 10:23a ESV). For me, this has been an important understanding of following Christ. I am free to do many things, but not everything I want to do is helpful to my goal of following Christ. I'm free to choose (with my personality, this is a key freedom), but I'm also free not to choose. Can I eat a row of Oreo cookies? Yes, I'm free to eat a row of Oreo cookies, but it probably won't help me achieve my goal of losing weight. Can I choose to be angry or bitter? Yes, those choices are within my power, but again, those choices don't help me. For some reason, viewing choices through the lens of helpful or not helpful is much easier for me than trying to keep the rules. If something doesn't help me be a better disciple of Christ, I choose not to do it. Whether the choice is good or bad doesn't matter; it's just not helpful, so I don't do it.

That leaves us with those things that do bring us closer to Christ. Again, there are no hard-and-fast rules. We're free in Christ to design our lives in ways that work best for us. If we are early birds, we're free to get up early and go to bed early. If we're night owls, fine. Stay up late and then sleep late. It doesn't matter. The reason I'm talking about this now is, for a long time, I confused what was required in Scripture with other people's opinions. In Scripture, there are a handful of commandments we must do. The rest we're free to figure out on our own. In fact, Jesus pulled all the commands of God into two: love God with everything you are and love your neighbor as yourself (my translation). That's it. Now, there's no law that says I have to go to church. If I love Jesus, however, I will love being with his people because Jesus himself loves being with his people. How I express that is up to me. I can join a mega church. I can join a house church. That's not going to be something that Jesus is concerned about. Did I love him? Did I love my neighbor? Did I love myself?

That brings us closer to our purpose. Simon Sinek, in his book, *Start with Why*,[10] writes that great leaders provide clarity for their organizations and those who work for them. By beginning with "why," the rest of the questions begin to make sense. Adam is introduced into God's story as a steward. In Genesis chapter 2, God gives Adam a garden. God doesn't give Adam the whole world, just a garden. Adam was charged to work in the garden and tend to it. Adam's job was to work so the garden fulfilled all of God's expectations. In the same way, we are called to be stewards with the moments and opportunities we work within so all of the kingdom potential within them is fulfilled. We get to be part of God's work as he redeems his world in small and big ways. There are no small jobs. All of creation is going to be brought back into the original plan and dream of God, and we get to be part of that. This is our "why." We're called to redeem every moment God

10. Simon Sinek, *Start with Why: How Great Leaders Inspire Everyone to Take Action* (New York: Portfolio/Penguin, 2009, 2011).

places us in—our families, our friends, our communities and neighborhoods.

How we do this is largely up to us. Want to teach children? God bless you. Want to work with the homeless? God bless you too. The opportunities and callings are as varied as we are. Find the place where you thrive. Find the place where you see Jesus at work. Find the place where you see the kingdom of God breaking through. Don't let anyone else's opinion become a law for you. We have a lot of freedom in Christ. Live in it.

What happens if we fail? We get back up and try again. Failing is part of the human experience. Remember when you learned to walk? Okay, you don't remember, but let's stay with the point. When we were learning to walk, we fell. We fell a lot. We would take a step and fall. We would take two steps and fall. The goal of walking was to extend the times between falling. Following Jesus is difficult. It's one of the reasons more people don't follow him. It's hard. This means we're going to fail. When we do, confess what you need to confess and get going again. Life is too short to wallow in failure.

Jesus invites us to test him. He wants us to try out his teachings. He's convinced his way is the best way. When I was in college, every class seemed to have a lab. There would be lectures for three hours a week, and then at least one afternoon a week, students would attend a lab to do experiments or exercises to reinforce the truth of the lectures. Biology would have lectures about the life systems of animals. Later that day, we'd go to the lab and see the life systems by dissecting the animal of the week (worms, frogs, mussels, etc.). Botany would have lectures and labs filled with plants. Language studies would have lectures where you learned nouns and verbs, and then labs where students would speak the subject language and hear how the correct pronunciation actually sounded. Each subject would have a chance to talk about the subject and then a lab experience where the lecture is validated.

Life is the same way. The lecture/lab structure isn't as obvious, but it works the same way. We go to church or small groups and listen to the teachings of Jesus. We hear the teacher talk about how a soft answer turns away wrath. We agree that sounds nice, but we don't think it will work. We leave the discipleship lesson, and on our way home, we get caught in a construction zone. We're patiently inching our car along in the traffic when another car comes zooming past us and now is angrily edging over into our lane. Now, we have a choice. Do we let them over? That would be the Christlike thing to do, but if you're like me (okay, I'm probably being too honest) you don't want to let them over. You want them to wait behind you. After all, that's only fair. Then, you remember the lesson. So, your version of the soft answer is to slow up and let the other driver over. Does it work? Surprisingly, yes. Our blood pressure drops, there's no stress, and we continue on our way. But the rude driver won! So? Does it matter? Did we lose anything important to us? Probably not.

This brings us to the most important aspect of following Christ—our identity. The reason nothing important is at risk in these everyday kinds of moments is because who we are is secure in Christ. We are loved. We didn't do anything to deserve it. We can't earn it. In Christ, God has offered us his unfathomable, eternal love for us. We are valued by God, which means we're eternally valued. That someone else doesn't value us doesn't diminish us at all. We are known. We are at home with Christ. We aren't valued because of what we have or what we've done. The world values us for such things. We're valued because of who we are.

How different would our lives be if we lived every moment not having to prove anything to anybody? We don't have to earn anyone's love. We're fully loved already. We don't have to prove our value. We're valued already. We don't have to look for meaning in our lives because we know our purpose. We don't have to be afraid of what's coming next. Our God has already walked millions through the valley of death. He can get us through as well. The hardest thing about learning how to swim is to learn to float. The most difficult thing to teach a child as they are learning how to swim is how to relax and trust the water. Once the child learns how to float, it's easy to add the strokes and the kicks. What if each one of us could learn how to float in our lives? What if we could just relax and trust Jesus to hold us up the way the water holds up a swimmer?

Like I said earlier, Christianity makes the claim that living as a disciple of Christ is the best way to live. So, let's give it a try. After all, life is the laboratory of faith. Don't think the ways of Jesus will work? Give them a try. I'm serious. Here's what I've found out about Jesus. He understands our humanity. There are days when all we have is all we have. We'd love to do more, believe more, trust more, but right now, this handful of faith is all we have. Jesus will take that. Do what you do in the moment as if you believed in Jesus with all your heart. You don't have to be perfect. You just have to do your best in the moment. Jesus will understand this is your best effort, and he will understand the weakness of our faith. Remember, Jesus only asks for faith the size of a mustard seed. Have you ever seen a mustard seed? They look like a dot that a ballpoint pen would make on a piece of paper. That's all the faith, Jesus said, that is necessary to move a mountain. Jesus will take your smallest efforts and multiply them into miracles. The feeding of the five thousand started with a little boy's lunch. Jesus can work with smaller faith than this.

I believe Jesus will show up in your life if you give him half a chance. Give it a try. Labs are where we prove the truth of what we've heard in a lecture. Life is when we prove the truth of what Jesus told us. There's no better way to live and Jesus is proof. Our calling as pastors is to get this conversation started. We're there to help our friends take the first step. How do we create safe places in our churches for people to try out Jesus's teaching? I can hear the reaction now. "You're either all in with Jesus or you're not in at all." I agree. My point is no one starts all in. Most of us dip our toe in the water before we dive in. Most of us taste a bite before we eat the entire dish. Churches should be places where our friends can "taste the Lord" and find out for themselves how good he is.

Chapter 10

Life-on-Life Preaching

I remember when I bought my first mobile phone. No, it wasn't a smartphone. It was just a phone. All it did was call other phones. There were no apps, no internet. Just dial seven numbers (you didn't even have to dial the area code in those days), and you could talk to someone on their phone. But you couldn't talk long. It was too expensive. The phone came in a leather carrying case the size of a small briefcase. The phone was so large it was soon nicknamed a "brick phone." Now, our phones are so small, we carry them with us everywhere in the palm of our hands. We now have more computing power in our phones than the NASA astronauts did when they landed on the moon.

Everything is getting smaller. Computers that once took up entire floors of buildings now sit on our desktops. Cars are smaller. We no longer have the solid steel behemoths with massive V-8 engines. Now we drive "compacts." Offices are getting smaller and "tiny homes" are becoming more and more popular. These days, you can buy a tiny house on the internet and have it all set up in a few days. The homes are amazing, we're told, and yes, you can live comfortably in a few hundred square feet. Everything in our lives now is "mini," "digitized," or "tiny." Even our clothing is being redesigned to accommodate all the gadgets we now want to carry in our pockets. Armies are getting smaller. No longer are battles fought by thousands of men and hundreds of armored vehicles. Now, battles are fought by small, highly trained units that can be inserted into a battlefield through fast, mobile vehicles.

Churches are getting smaller too. There are a couple of reasons for this. First, building costs have increased to place a lot of building projects out of reach for church. Second, millennials and Gen Xers won't pay for expensive building projects. These upcoming generations give, but they give very differently than previous generations. A common myth among church leaders is that the younger generations don't give. This isn't true. They do give and they give generously, but before they give, millennials, Gen Xers, and Generation Alpha need to see a direct correlation from their giving to the impact they're making. If they can't make that connection, they won't give.

Several years ago, our church had outgrown our facilities. The common wisdom of the day was to make plans to enlarge the sanctuary to accommodate more and more people. We decided not to enlarge the sanctuary; instead, we decided to start more churches. Instead of expecting people to come to us, we tried to place a church in their neighborhoods. We called them "FOBS." This is a military term for "forward operating bases." The idea is to put combat units close to where the enemy is. It's the same concept for churches. We wanted to put churches close to the people we wanted to reach. When we started hearing comments such as, "My neighbors say the church is too far away," or, "We want our kids to go to church with kids they go to school with," we knew it was time to start a new church.

We've found the following numbers to be relevant in any new church start. The first number is 150. This is the number a church has to average in attendance to be a sustainable congregation. An attendance of 150 every Sunday would mean a congregation of at least 600 people, given the attendance patterns in our churches these days. The other number is 500. An average attendance of 500 every Sunday means the congregation has about 2,000 members or more. This number is sufficient to support beginning another church. While this isn't a hard-and-fast number, by this stage of the congregation's life, a couple of things should be happening. First, a planting pastor should have been identified and started preparation for leading the new church. Second, a community should have been identified and small groups should have been started that will become part of the new church plant. If the new church plant starts averaging 500 in attendance, they will begin the process of planting another church, and so on and so forth.

Small, agile, and tightly focused on their local neighborhoods—and more important, focused on their neighbors—the whole world is reached by each person reaching out to the person closest to them. Consider the first stories of the early church. Philip hears Jesus and goes to find Nathaniel. Andrew hears Jesus and goes to find Peter. Barnabas, after his split with Paul, goes to Cyprus. (Barnabas was from Cyprus.) When the early church faces persecution, a lot of Jewish Christians move to Antioch. Barnabas goes to check out the reports of how the new church is flourishing and ends up bringing Paul to Antioch. Everything is based on relationships. I know a guy who knows a guy, and before you know it, the whole world is reached with the gospel of Jesus Christ.

It's the gospel's version of "Six Degrees of Separation." There used to be a parlor game where you would try to connect people all over the world by whom they were related to or whom they had worked with. The most popular version of this game was focused on the actor Kevin Bacon. According to those who played this game often, Kevin Bacon could be connected to just about anyone in the world by working through six generations of relationships. Maybe the world isn't that big after all.

I'm not saying we don't support mission efforts to carry the gospel around the world. I know many people who have the necessary gifts to be good missionaries. They adapt easily to change. They're comfortable in different cultures. In fact, they are delighted to explore the world and witness God's creation. Most of us don't have these gifts. We're not cut out for mission work within different cultures. We're called to reach our neighbors who, in turn, will reach their neighbors.

And who is our neighbor? Believe it or not, we're not the first ones to ask that question. In Luke 10:25–27, Jesus is questioned by an expert in the law. Jesus's answer prompts another question: "Who is my neighbor?" (v. 29). Jesus answers the question by telling the story of the Good Samaritan. Everyone knows the story. A man is on his way from Jerusalem to Jericho and is jumped by robbers who steal everything he has and beat him. The robbers leave the man half dead, laying in the middle of the road. A priest and a Levite travel by, see the man, and each walks to the other side of the road and neither one of them does anything to help the man. A Samaritan comes by, sees the man, and helps him. He tends to the wounded man and takes him to a nearby inn to recover, promising to pay for his care when the Samaritan returns.

"So, who is the neighbor?" Jesus asked. "The one who stopped," was the answer. Jesus changed the question from "Who is my neighbor?" to "Am I a good neighbor?" Short answer: my neighbor is the person in need who's closest to me. That could be on my street, in my church, or in my own house. This means every Christian home is the inn on the road where wounded people recover.

When I began my ministry, like many others, Billy Graham was my hero. To be able to preach with such passion and conviction to thousands of people who filled the stadiums of the crusades was my dream. In fact, it was the dream of most of the pastors I knew. Few of us, however, had the gifting and anointing to be able to do that. We were the pastors of neighborhood congregations and suburban churches who served bigger sections of a city. For those of us who were paying attention, we could see the signs several years ago. There was a revolt against "bigness." People stopped shopping at large grocery store chains and found farmer's markets to buy their food. Knowing who provided your food, who grew the crops and butchered the cows, suddenly became a thing. Restaurant chains were abandoned for local eateries. Schools were celebrated not for their innovative techniques, but for their small class sizes, where individual attention could be found in small student-to-teacher ratios.

While these trends had started earlier, the Covid-19 pandemic took it to a whole new level. People lost trust in every public institution. People no longer trusted the government at any level—local, state, or federal. Doctors were doubted. Their integrity and knowledge were questioned by their patients. Every doctor's diagnosis was challenged by something somebody had read on Google. Church leaders were questioned by members who wanted to know the foundations of every decision. Who had told us that masks would stop the virus? Did the government have the authority to shut down our worship services? Neighbors disagreed with neighbors and friendships were lost, depending on what side each one took on how best to deal with the pandemic. For a while it seemed that no one trusted anyone.

Gradually, as people started to return to their normal lives, they slowly began to extend their trust, but only a little bit at a time. Big institutions are still suspect. Large churches are too. This lack of trust was only exacerbated when several well-known pastors were forced to step down because of moral failures or other disqualifying behaviors. If people were going to go to church, they wanted to know their pastors, and they wanted to know them well enough to validate their character.

I tell pastors they preach their most important sermons long before they reach the pulpit, and it happens as a congregation watches their pastors walk around the congregation. Does the pastor speak to members? Is there a genuine concern from the pastor toward the church members? How does the pastor treat his wife? Their children? Every member of the congregation assumes that if the pastor doesn't treat his own family well, he won't treat them well either.

Recently, a friend of mine left a position with a well-known megachurch and started a house church. He had been discipling several of his friends and neighbors in a small group and decided he wanted to do this full-time. When I talked to him over lunch one day, he was genuinely excited to be doing church this way. He talked about how they get together as a large group once a month for worship and a shared meal. They celebrate their joys and share their sorrows. They meet weekly in small groups and, as he described it, there's always some kind of gathering happening within the church. Moms get together for play dates with children and Bible study. Older professional men mentor the younger men who are just getting started in their careers. To hear him describe it, they're doing church all the time. Whenever a person is recognized by the church as a leader, they are encouraged to start a church in their home. In our last conversation, he mentioned they had five new house churches going.

In learning about his work establishing house churches, our conversation focused on the centrality of the table in the Christian faith. Hospitality has been a key ingredient in the growth of Christianity from the beginning. Remember

Butterfield's story? Her conversion journey centered around the table in Pastor Ken Smith's home. This so impacted Butterfield that her next book was titled *The Gospel Comes with a House Key.*[11] According to Butterfield, the gospel is best shared when it is lived out around a kitchen table. As meals and stories are shared, people find a safe place to begin to deal with their flaws and mistakes. Gradually, and I do mean gradually, walls come down, and over countless dinners, people see another way to live.

They just don't know how to get there. No one does. Sooner or later, everyone needs a coach, a mentor, or a guide. Donald Miller, the well-known author and life coach, writes: "To me, becoming a guide is the most meaningful transformation that can happen in a human life."[12] For Miller, the best use of our lives is to help someone who is behind us on the journey. Once you come to a place of maturity in your own life, circle back to those who are just starting in their lives. I would tell senior adults don't join another Sunday school class or small group for senior adults. Instead, join a young adults class or group. Spend time with young married couples. Let them see what a marriage of forty-plus years looks like. Share with them the painful lessons learned over the years so these young adults can gain this wisdom without having to go through the painful lesson from which the wisdom is learned.

---

11. Rosaria Butterfield, *The Gospel Comes with a House Key: Practicing Radically Ordinary Hospitality in Our Post-Christian World* (Wheaton, IL: Crossway, 2018), 74.
12. Donald Miller, *Hero on a Mission: A Path to a Meaningful Life* (New York: HarperCollins, 2022), 15.

In the dramatic moments after the Lord's Supper, Jesus tells Peter, "Simon, Simon, look out. Satan has asked to sift you like wheat. But I have prayed for you that your faith may not fail. And you, when you have turned back, strengthen your brothers" (Luke 22:31–32). Note Jesus's final instruction to Peter: once you've gotten through this, Peter, turn back and help your brothers. Our calling isn't to be sure we alone get to heaven, but we're called to make sure all of our brothers and sisters make it as well.

Before my retirement from my role as senior pastor of Brentwood Baptist Church, I was spending most of my time working with our campus pastors. As I told them, "I learned to pastor a church from old guys, and now, I am the old guy!" There is so much about leadership in the local church that no one teaches you. Once graduated from seminary, a pastor thinks they're ready to lead a church. They're not. There is a broad set of skills a pastor must learn in order to effectively lead. Unfortunately, too many of our young pastors learn these lessons through trial and error. That is a brutally painful way to learn. Having an experienced pastor as a coach or mentor is a much better use of life.

When I was working with these young pastors, we would watch the videos of their sermons. We would talk about how the shrinking attention span of American adults has affected preaching. The adult attention span is about twenty minutes. We don't have to like that fact, but we do have to acknowledge it. Preaching for forty-five minutes doesn't seem to work anymore. People will stop listening after twenty minutes and start processing what they've heard in the first twenty minutes of the sermon. They aren't taking in any new information. Like it or not, that's the reality we live in. Novels have fewer pages. Magazine articles have fewer words. People don't have the attentive capacity to handle more.

How do you visit a member in the hospital? Yes, it's better to tell the nurse you're on the floor and always knock and announce yourself—even when the door is open. If you don't, you run the risk of you and your church member sharing an experience neither one of you wants. How do you do a funeral? A baptism? Saying the right words at the right moment is only part of the pastor's duty. Walking a family through this part of the journey requires an ability to listen to what's not being said in the moment. This kind of education only comes over a few cups of coffee listening to a more experienced pastor share what they've learned over the years.

I spent a lot of time talking to the young pastors about the basics. If a pastor is going to succeed over the long haul, they will have to doggedly protect their spiritual practices. Bible study and prayer cannot be skipped, ignored, or rushed. Ministry, however you express, comes out of the overflow of Christ's presence in your life. Without this overflow, not only can you not do your ministry well, you become dangerous to your ministry. Ministers don't explode. We implode. The pressure on the outside—expectations of church members, preaching a sermon every seven days, managing the church's finances—becomes greater than the pressure on the inside, and we are crushed like a cheap soda can. Helping a young pastor understand how important their prayer life is becomes a challenge because every young pastor feels intense pressure to do something. It takes a while to help them understand that the vitality of their ministry is founded in who they are, not necessarily in what they do.

Every pastor should be training the next generation of leaders. Look at the ministries of Jesus and Paul. For all of Jesus's work with the multitudes that followed him, most of his time was spent with the twelve disciples, and much of that time was with John, James, and Peter. Paul made sure to train Timothy and Titus. In Paul's letters to Timothy and Titus, you would think the letters would be about evangelism and theology. Instead, the letters are about leadership. These are the people you should choose as leaders, Paul writes, and here are the qualifications you should seek. Every leader should be training a leader. Every pastor should be training a pastor.

Several years ago, I told the church this story. "Let me tell you how the future will come," I told them. "One of you will come up to me and ask me if I remembered telling our congregation to stay home and see what our neighbors did on Sunday morning. You'll say, 'My wife and I ended up talking to our friends as they walked their dogs.' Then you will tell me that you started talking to them about attending a Bible study. 'They loved the idea and my neighbors said they would love to come over to our house for that. But when? Guess what? None of my neighbors are busy on Sunday morning.'"

The old me would have tried to get all those people to attend our church. The new me will train the church member who's hosting their neighbors to be a pastor. The twenty-five or so neighbors who show up to share life and brunch may be the future of the church. I know. All the experts are pointing to the demise of the church, but the church won't die. First of all, Jesus promised it wouldn't, and second of all, the genius of the church is the ability to adapt. Churches in China survive by doing church one way. The church in Europe survives by doing church another way. The church in America may survive by going back to the models that were so successful in the first-century church.

Conversations in restaurants and in homes, making disciples over dinner—these are the practices that have always worked. They're the same ones that will work now. Find a guide. Get a mentor. Be a guide. Be a mentor. It's the way the future has always happened.

Chapter 11

A Whole New World

I remember watching Jackie Gleason in a movie called *Gigot* when I was a child. It's a comedy film made in 1962, and Gleason plays a mute who lives in the basement of his landlady's apartment building. He squeezes out a meager living working as a janitor and doing odd jobs around his neighborhood in Paris. Early in the movie, Gigot finds a woman and her young daughter huddled in a doorway, trying to keep out of the rain. Gigot brings the woman and her daughter to his small basement apartment and, over time, becomes very fond of the little girl. When he takes her to church, he realizes Nicole, the little girl, has no understanding of God or church. Frustrated by his inability to communicate with her, he begins to slap himself in the face. Nicole finally calms Gigot by showing she's beginning to understand.

I saw that movie over fifty years ago and, for some reason, as I started thinking about preaching to our post-truth world, I remembered Gigot's frustration for his inability to communicate the great things of God to the little girl. Like Gigot, I felt as if I was mute, trying to communicate the glory of God and the wonders of his love to a group of people who didn't understand God's language at all. I could describe the story of God in theological terms. I could lay out the philosophical foundations for the existence of God and the reliability of the Bible. What I couldn't do was help my friends see the difference, the real difference, Jesus could make in their lives. In church, we talk a lot about when Jesus will return and how it will be in heaven. What we don't talk enough about is how Jesus is with us now and how much better life is when we live in his presence.

With us? How? Through the ministry of his Spirit. Remember, Jesus promised his Spirit would walk alongside us and continue to teach us the ways of Jesus. The Spirit would be our encourager, our teacher, and if needed, our disciplinarian. When things get hard, the Spirit will give us strength. When we are confused, he will give us wisdom. When the storms threaten to sink our little boats, he will be the anchor that holds us fast. Why couldn't I find the words?

Well, because we don't start with words. We start with silence. All the great conversations begin with silence. We start with the silence that comes from a heartache that can't be spoken in words. This heartache can only be expressed in the deep sighs of prayer and meditation. In the long moments when we bring the names of our friends before the Lord and ask for some way to reach them. This process begins with a heartache. When I was younger, it wasn't unusual for pastors to break down in their sermons, overcome with concern for their lost neighbors and friends. Pastors don't cry that much anymore. Maybe we should start.

In chapter 9 of his Gospel, Matthew records one of the most poignant moments in Scripture. Jesus is observing the crowds that are following him, and as he looks at them, his heart begins to break. They are like sheep without a shepherd. Jesus was deeply moved (the Greek terms can be roughly translated "he felt compassion for them down in his bones"). Jesus is so moved that he asks the disciples to pray that the Lord of the harvest will send workers to the field. I've always found it interesting that Jesus, the Son of God, would ask his disciples to pray. Not only was Jesus asking the original Twelve to pray, but he was also asking us to pray. In a weird way, we're now the laborers Jesus prayed for being sent into the field.

Our work always begins with a burden. Pastors have known this for a long time. Sermons always begin with a burden. At least, the good ones do. Some sermons are preached simply because it's Sunday morning and the preacher has to say something, but the best sermons start as dull aches in the chest, like a toothache in the soul that won't go away. They start as small pricks in the preacher's consciousness. Perhaps the preacher will hear something in a conversation. No one else will notice it, but the preacher won't be able to forget the little lie that went unchallenged. Only the preacher's ears will catch the false teaching that was quickly assumed to be true by everyone else around the table. The preacher will try to pass it off, saying to themselves that they can't fix everything, that they can't talk about everything. So, they'll just try to let it go.

As we've tried to professionalize the ministry, we've lost some of the urgency in our preaching. Too many pastors never preach with a broken heart. There's no urgency in the call, no desperation in the words. This heartache can't be manufactured in the moment of the sermon. The preacher isn't an actor performing an entertaining monologue. The pastor is a witness. The pastor is someone who knows what can be but must live with what is.

Now, more and more Christians know the frustration of trying to speak God into a world that doesn't recognize God. Again, they aren't hostile to us or our message. They're indifferent. If God exists, fine, and if he doesn't, that's fine too. God, for them, is like someone who lives in the neighborhood they haven't met yet. Whether God's here or not makes no real difference to the decisions they make every day. And this bothers us. What's more, it keeps on bothering us.

The discomfort grows and the dull ache in our hearts won't let us rest. The more intense our prayer and Bible study, the more the weight of the burden grows. We will become more and more aware of the gap. The gap between how our friends and neighbors could be living and how they actually live. The difference between what could be and what actually is. Most people live lives way below their potential and possibilities. They become trapped by the consequences of poor decisions, held hostage by fears and demeaning pronouncements by people who held power in their lives. Some have been abused or abandoned. Others have simply given up. These people feel like the life they wanted is no longer possible for them. If we're still enough for long enough, we'll feel their despair.

Some in our congregation respond in anger. They believe that they deserve to have what others have and they're determined to take it regardless of the cost. They strike out, blaming others for their frustrations and failures. One fight just starts another. And even if the prize is won, they quickly discover whatever trophy they have brought home from their conquest isn't really worth having. So, another fight is started and another and another, until there is no one left to fight. The gap continues to grow. The gap between what kind of life is possible and what kind of life is actually lived. Men and women go to work and come home. They make plenty of money, but no matter how much money they make, it's never enough. Children make good grades, but they never receive the encouragement they need. People seek peace to only find numbness. The harder we try, the larger the gap grows.

Soon, the pastor can no longer live with the pain of the growing gap and realizes something must be said. The moment will come when something has to be said. When a word of warning must be said or the preacher is a coward. When a word of hope must be proclaimed or the preacher doesn't believe. Something has to be said because that's the only way meaning is found. When an inner beast is named, it can now be confronted and conquered. When a past sin is spoken in confession, it can be forgiven. The word must be found. The word must be spoken. The gap must be closed.

The first step after prayer—much prayer—is to help our friends see there is a gap. There is a gap between the life they're living and the life that is possible in Christ. There is more to life—much more. There is a better way to live, and the name of that Way is Jesus. The first step is to help our friends understand there's a gap to begin with. How can the preacher close the gap between what can be and what is if no one believes there's a gap in the first place? What if no one believes there is a better way? What if no one believes in what could be? What if they're convinced that all there is might be all there is?

To do this, we have to crawl into the gap between the lives our friends are living and the lives they want to live. Our friends want better and deeper marriages, but they don't know how to build marriages like that. Too many of our friends grew up in broken marriages or single-parent homes. Young men are trying to be good husbands and they've never seen a husband. Young women are trying to be good wives and they've never seen one. How can you be a good parent if you didn't have good parents? How can those stories be rewritten? How can we change how the stories end? Are we chained to the destiny of the narratives we were born into? Trapped by our own mistakes? In the power of Christ, no we aren't.

There is good news, but we will have to earn the right to share that good news. People have become jaded and suspicious of each other. Covid and the intense polarization of our nation has made even the most superficial conversations difficult. People don't trust each other. Why should they? Trust, today more than ever, has to be earned. We begin earning that trust by listening. We must listen deeply enough to hear the pain behind each word and to hear the silences of those things not spoken. One of the first things I learned in my ministry is that the reason people told me they needed to talk to me was rarely the reason they wanted to talk to me. Sometimes the reason people tell you they're angry isn't the reason they're angry, but you'll have to listen to the stories and, then, hear the story behind the story, to begin to understand.

Indeed, one of the highest callings we have is to give words to those things that can't be spoken. In the creation story, God gives Adam the ability to name the animals. One of our most important powers is the ability to name something. All of us have either had the frustration or know someone who had the same frustration of having symptoms, but no doctor is able to give a diagnosis. There is such a relief when the illness is finally named.

And we're called on to name the experience at all kinds of times. Friends gather for a funeral. Something about the deceased person's story makes the funeral one of those when no one knows what to say. Christ followers have words for that. We can speak light into darkness and hope into despair. The risen Christ gives us a new ending to all of our stories. Yet, it's more than that. Many of our heartaches have theological origins. That is, our suffering and pain have sin at their root, and we can't find healing until we deal with those roots. Most of us don't have a theological language to effectively name our pain. This, of course, means we can't find a remedy because we can't name the illness.

This sermon can't be preached from the pulpit in the sanctuary. There's no three points and a poem here. This conversation happens on the third hole of the golf course or the same booth for a Saturday morning breakfast. It happens in the boarding area of the airport—any place where the person we're with will feel safe enough to talk about what really matters in their lives. These conversations happen in the middle of our friends' lives. This is where every sermon has to be preached, where every gospel conversation has to happen. Not in exalted language, but in everyday language that can be understood by any fifth grader. These conversations are personal, up close, across a table or in conversations while walking—the sermons of the future won't just be preached on Sunday mornings, but in conversations every day of the week.

This doesn't happen when people go to church. This happens when the church goes to them and the pulpit is no longer at the front of the sanctuary, but in the middle of the world. Why? Because that's where the people are. Even a basic skimming of the New Testament will show us how few times Jesus spoke inside a formal religious structure. Jesus did speak at the temple and in several synagogues, but most of his conversations and sermons were in the open. He talked with Peter on the shores of Galilee. He talked with a woman at a well and Zacchaeus at the bottom of a tree. Jesus found Cleopas and his friend on the road to Emmaus, and Nicodemus visited Jesus in the middle of the night. One of the greatest worship services in history was led by Paul and Silas in a Philippian jail.

Why am I writing this? Because every denomination is beginning to see a decline in church attendance. For too many reasons to name, people aren't coming to church the way they once did. This trend became very evident during and after Covid-19. Recently, we've seen a rash of accusations against pastors and other religious leaders for inappropriate sexual behavior—everything from rape to sexual assault to inappropriate comments made in the workplace. What made it worse was the reaction of church leaders when these crimes were brought to light. When challenged with these awful realities, the institution of the church either ignored the reports or actually protected the accused. People gave up on the institution of the church.

The second reason people stopped coming to church is that families are overcommitted. From parents who are working sixty to seventy hours a week to children who are having to do homework after ballet lessons, piano lessons, the sport of the season practice, and other extra-curricular activities, Sunday mornings have become the only time the family can be home and relax. That's assuming, of course, one of the children isn't on a travel ball team. Church doesn't seem to be necessary to the average American family. The additional things the church used to provide such as friendships, social connections, and support during tough times are all found somewhere else.

In short, people aren't coming back to church. I hate to be the one to tell you this, but the United States isn't a Christian nation. We may have been founded on Judeo-Christian principles, but we no longer abide by those principles. *TIME* magazine produces a list of the one hundred most influential people every year. In this edition, they'll feature musicians and writers, politicians and activists, business leaders and computer geniuses. I can't remember the last time a religious leader was featured. I can't remember the last time a Christian was featured for living out their faith in our world. There are few Christian voices in the public square. Two thousand years later, we found ourselves right back where we started—a fringe group of society.

That's okay. Like I said, we've been here before. Some of the church's best stories come from that time in our history. We've got to think like our first-century brothers and sisters. We have to think like missionaries. How do we do that? Ask yourself this question: If someone from the churches in Jerusalem or Antioch visited your city, where would they start? *Probably, they'd start preaching in some local church.* Okay, do that. *They would seek out people of peace and share Jesus with them.* Okay, do that. *They would pray for the city.* Okay, do that. We're no longer chaplains of the status quo. We are either missionaries or we aren't anything at all.

Now, before we start wringing our hands about how our nation has turned away from God, let's remember there was a time when no one came to church. In the first century, what did the early church do? The church went to them. They met in people's homes. They met in local markets and town centers. They would talk to people. They would talk to anyone who was nearby. They would talk to Roman soldiers and jailers. They would talk to women in the marketplace. They would visit neighbors in their homes. They would, like Philip, go to a road in the middle of nowhere to meet an Ethiopian who was reading the Bible while he was traveling in a chariot.

Here's the bottom line: Jesus loves our neighbors and friends; therefore, we love them too. That means we'll have to find a way to make opportunities to talk to them about Jesus.

Why? Because knowing Jesus is the best way to live. Live in such a way, people become curious about your life. If the fruit of the Spirit is love, live in love. If it's joy and peace, live in joy and peace. Trust me, no one around you is living in joy and peace. Christ followers should be peculiar for our love, joy, peace, kindness, gentleness, and all the rest. We should be so filled with Christ we live in the overflow of his love for us. I know, a life like that is hard to explain. That's why it's better to live it than talk about it sometimes. When you stick out like that, people will want to know why.

Be ready to tell them the "why" is Jesus.

Nashville is filled with world-class musicians. As a rock and roll junkie, I've had the privilege of meeting some of the best players in the world. In getting to know these musicians, I've noticed a particular trait among the truly great ones: they love music—all kinds of music. Conga drums? They love conga drums and can probably tell you a song where the congas were featured in a solo. Or better, tell you a story about a producer who fought with the artists to bring in a conga player to make the song a hit. They will listen to any instrument played by anyone. World-famous keyboardists will watch with fascination as a child plays "Chopsticks" on a piano. Afterward, the musician will be the most excited fan of the child.

When I asked one of my friends how he could enjoy such amateurish efforts, he looked at me and smiled. "I'm listening for the joy," he said. "Any true musician," he said, "plays with joy. A child who's forced to take piano lessons plays very differently from a child who, while not as talented, loves the piano and plays with a fierce gusto." He went on: "It's the same with every musician. The great ones never lose their joy."

I know. Living as a Christ follower in these times can be almost impossible. Trying to find a sermon to reach someone in these cynical times can be heartbreakingly hard. Do it anyway. We may think we're never getting it right. We may get down on ourselves, thinking we should have said it better or used a different story. Don't worry about any of that. Just be you. Tell them what you know about Jesus. They're not listening to your words. They're listening for the joy.

Epilogue

I remember seeing her wait around after the Kairos service. Kairos was a Tuesday-night worship experience for young adults I led at Brentwood Baptist Church. We had just finished a teaching series on dealing with dysfunctional families, and I had told them to write a letter to their dads. "I don't care if all you write is: 'I don't want to hate you anymore,'" I told them. "Just write. And if you get stuck, come sit down with me and we'll talk." She circled around until there was no one else waiting to talk to me, and then she walked over and sat down with me. Her hands were trembling as she handed me a blank sheet of paper.

"My father started abusing me when I was seven years old," she said. "What do I write?" I was stunned by her vulnerability. I was speechless as I saw the pain and fear in her eyes. We talked about how it wasn't her fault and that she wouldn't be able to walk out of this valley without a trained guide, and we helped her get into counseling. That's what happened to her.

Here's what happened to me. I remember leaving the building and walking to my car. I remember telling myself to get to my car, and *then* I could fall apart. I remember getting in my car and placing my forehead against the steering wheel and losing it. I cried as I prayed, "I don't know what to do. I don't know how to help. But, Lord Jesus, if you'll tell me what to do, I'll die trying to get it done."

That moment changed my life. That moment changed my preaching. As you come to the end of this book, I'm praying you have such a moment. I hope your life is wrecked when you understand the confusion and despair that grips our congregations and neighbors. I pray you are wrecked by grief when you realize how many lives are broken and how many of our friends are wounded because no one loved them enough to tell them the truth.

Despite all the naysayers, I'm very optimistic about the church and the church's future in Christ. For one thing, Jesus promised the church would be able to withstand whatever hell threw against it. And second, I'm talking to more and more preachers who understand the hopelessness of our world can't be healed by any human effort, no matter how sophisticated or well planned. This *has* to be a work of God. When this reality hits us as preachers, we're desperate to release the Spirit in our congregations and to see the grace of Jesus released in our neighborhoods—so much so that we'd pay any price to see it happen. We'd die trying to see it happen.

When you have that moment, let me know. When you preach that sermon, call me. I want to be there when you do.

About the Author

Dr. Mike Glenn is president of The Engage Church Network and former senior pastor of Brentwood Baptist Church. Under his leadership, the church has grown to nine campuses and a membership of well over 10,000. Mike Glenn has written three books—*In Real Time*, *The Gospel of Yes*, and *Coffee with Mom*. Glenn is married to his wife Jeannie. When he is not equipping pastors, Glenn is spending time with his wife and keeping up with his grandchildren.